THE WATTS TOWERS

Leon Whiteson

Photographs
by
Marvin Rand

MOSAIC PRESS
Oakville - New York - London

CANADIAN CATALOGUING IN PUBLICATION DATA

Whiteson, Leon, 1930-
  The Watts Towers

Bibliography: p.
ISBN 0-88962-394-5 (bound). - ISBN 0-88962-393-7 (pbk.)

1. Rodia, Simon. 2. Watts Towers (Los Angeles, Calif.).
3. Assemblage (Art) - California - Los Angeles.
4. Watts (Los Angeles, Calif.) - Buildings, structures,
etc. I. Title.

N6537.R6A78 1988   725'.97'0979494   C88-094810-8

No part of this book may be reproduced or transmitted in any form, by any means, electronic or mechanical, including photocopying and recording information storage and retrieval systems, without permission in writing from the publisher, except by a reviewer who may quote brief passages in a review.

Published by MOSAIC PRESS, P.O. Box 1032, Oakville, Ontario, L6J 5E9, Canada. Offices and warehouse at 1252 Speers Road, Units# 1&2, Oakville, Ontario, L6L 5N9, Canada.

Mosaic Press acknowledges the assistance of the Canada Council and the Ontario Arts Council in support of its publishing programme.

Copyright©Leon Whiteson, 1989
Design by Rita Vogel
Cover Design by Rita Vogel

Printed and bound in Hong Kong

ISBN 0-88962-393-7 PAPER
ISBN 0-88962-394-5 CLOTH

MOSAIC PRESS:
In Canada:
        MOSAIC PRESS, 1252 Speers Road, Units# 1&2, Oakville, Ontario L6J 5N9, Canada.
              P.O. Box 1032, Oakville, Ontario L6J 5E9

In the United States:
        Kampman National Book Network Inc., 4720-A, Boston Way, Lanham, MO., 20706,
              USA

In the U.K.:
        John Calder (Publishers) Ltd., 18 Brewer Street, London, W1R 4A5, England

TABLE OF CONTENTS

I. Foreword: Los Angeles Mayor, Tom Bradley, 5

II. Introduction: Charles Moore, 7

III. Sam Rodia and His Watts Towers: Leon Whiteson, 9

IV. Watts Leon Whiteson, 31

V. A Tour of the Towers: Bud & Arloa Goldstone, 41

VI. Children & the Watts Towers Arts Center: Rochelle Nicholas, Arts Center Program Coordinator, 47

'Sabato Alone:' John Outterbridge, Director, Watts Towers Art Center, 51

Los Angeles Schools' Watts Towers Competition, May, 1985, 52

VII. The Towers as Art: Christopher Knight, Art Critic, 55

VIII. The Musicians of Watts: Mikal Gilmore, Music Critic, 59

APPENDICES:

A   Conservation Challenges: Bud Goldstone, 67

B   The International Forum for the Future of Sam Rodia's Towers in Watts, June 13-15, 1985, 79

C   Chronology of the Towers, 1921 to 1987, 82

D   Bibliography, 87

Principal Photographer: Marvin Rand.

Other photographic sources:

Herald Examiner archives.

Trust archives.

Mabel Boyd, Willie Middlebrook, D.J. Robinson.

Index, 95

CITY HALL
LOS ANGELES,
CALIFORNIA 90012
(213) 485-3311

OFFICE OF THE MAYOR
TOM BRADLEY
MAYOR

March 5, 1987

Leon Whiteson
Herald Examiner
1111 South Broadway
Los Angeles, California 90017

Dear Mr. Whiteson:

The Watts Towers represent a unique and important chapter in the history of Los Angeles: They stand both as a monument to the indomitable spirit of one man and as a symbol of hope for an entire community.

Sam Rodia, creator of the Towers, had a vision. An uneducated immigrant from Italy, Rodia labored as an unskilled construction worker by day. But at night and on weekends, come rain or come shine, he toiled in pursuit of his dream. He received assistance, financial or otherwise, from no one. Finally, after more than 30 years, Rodia completed his masterpiece.

Rodia named his assemblage of towers "Nuestro Pueblo," or "Our Town." But shortly after his finished the project, he left Los Angeles and never again laid eyes on his life's work. Still, the Towers stand as a legacy of hope to Watts.

Rodia faced great obstacles in the construction of his walled collection of pinnacles. But he never gave up. And after more than three decades of hard work and enormous sacrifice, Rodia completed what critics call an important work of art — even though he had no formal education or artistic training. Rodia built from plans etched only in his heart and in his mind.

The Watts Towers are a lasting symbol of Rodia's talent and tenacity. So, too, they give identity to a community known more for arson than for art. The tumultuous uprisings that rocked Watts in the early 1960s are history. And while problems remain, the past two decades have seen great progress.

-more-

AN EQUAL EMPLOYMENT OPPORTUNITY
-AFFIRMATIVE ACTION EMPLOYER"

Since 1965, we have built two health centers, six new housing developments with over 500 units, the $12 million Watts Shopping Center, Martin Luther King, Jr. Hospital, several senior citizens' centers and the Westminster Neighborhood Association Center. More community improvement projects are planned for the coming years.

The Towers represent the past, the present and the future of Watts. And just as the people of the community have rallied to save the Towers from being condemned and destroyed, we are determined to rebuild Watts and fan the flames of hope that have given us Sam Rodia and others like him.

Sincerely,

TOM BRADLEY
MAYOR

CHARLES MOORE

Simon Rodia's towers in Watts resonate at once with the unschooled but deeply felt energies of the man who made them, and with some of the most venerable folk traditions in the world. The act of love which made these magnificent objects lasted a long time and scaled great heights. Sabbatino Rodia did it all, *suspended on a window washer's seat,* and pointed out later that he couldn't use any help, because he didn't know what he was going to do next himself.

Now any act of love which continues unabated for 30 years has a supernatural intensity to it which is seen by some of us as the very basis for art, but by many others as abnormal behaviour, in need of repression or elimination. So in 1957 the forces of urban renewal decided the Towers were unsafe, and should be pulled down. Fortunately, extensive demolition efforts were futile, and we still have the wonders preserved.

Then there is the other part of this wonder, its place in a lively worldwide folk tradition. A few decades earlier in Barcelona, Gaudi and Jujol had been breaking crockery, too, and affixing the shards to the curved surfaces of their buildings and the Guell Park. And towers have been built as memorials to a dream in many places, at many times. But Sam Rodia worked out this dream in Los Angeles at the very time that America's most dazzling form of popular art - the movies - was in its heyday. There is much in common between that world of fantasy on the silver screen that gave respite to Angelenos hemmed in by the great Depression, and Rodia's world of fantasy on spidery metal forms that gave him release from his troubles: both present whole worlds encapsulated in a story or a small suburban lot; both present an order in reality, from which we may (to borrow from T.S. Eliot) divine the order of reality. Because both are *real*, as real as our memories and our dreams and ourselves.

Charles Moore
March, '87

A non-profit corporation since 1959, informally known as "the towers committee," whose by-laws charge its members with the preservation and protection of the Towers of Simon Rodia in Watts.

III

SAM RODIA
AND
HIS TOWERS
Leon
Whiteson

From the top of the tallest of the Watts Towers, ninety nine and a half feet high at its peak, you look out over a landscape of hot streets with small bungalows that recall the semi-rural urban village of the 1920s and '30s where Sam Rodia built his visionary architectures.

Here you feel lifted above it all, way above the striving and the suffering of this troubled, energetic city of Los Angeles. You feel as Rodia must have felt when, pausing to rest his smallboned, wiry weight on the iron bar wrapped around his waist and hooked to a tower rung, feet steady on a cement rib, he tipped the sweaty old fedora back on his brow and gazed out over the flatland far below.

Power pylons march across the middle distance to the north, their silvery spires mimicking the slender potency and grace of the tower beneath you. In this trough in the Los Angeles basin the horizon is fuzzy. Cars glitter like beetles in the blurred sunshine. A horn sounds in the hot afternoon, a dog barks, a woman shouts for her child. A long string of Southern Pacific boxcars ambles among the houses.

You look down through your shoes at Rodia's masterwork. It is a collection of three tall spires, four smaller pinnacles, several fountains and fonts, a lacy gazebo roofed with open curved ribs, the ruins of a burnt-out cottage. The rounded tops of an encircling wall mark the boundaries of the triangular lot that, from up here, has the prowed thrust of a ship's deck. Rodia inscribed the name "Nuestro Pueblo" - Our Town - on his Towers, and it has the look of a miniature walled city.

Gazing directly down through the open web of the tower under you, you see that it is made up of concentric ribs linked by slender vertical legs tied together by radial spokes. Circular hoops widen from the narrow peak to which you cling down to a base that seems ridiculously slight to anchor such soaring spires.

Watts Train Station in the 1920's when Rodia was starting his Towers

The tallest tower is the western one. The central spire, a few feet lower, is joined to its 57-foot neighbor to the east by a series of delicate horizontals that brace them both. The smaller pinnacles are way below, only 15 to 30 feet high. All this is crowded into a triangular space 151 feet long on its hypoteneuse, 69 feet wide at its base, 137 feet along its side on 1765 107th St. E. This cluster of extraordinary structures seems like an upthrust of organic crystals bubbling out of the barren wasteland beside a disused rail corridor which has lost its tracks.

At ground level, seen in silhouette against the whitish Angeleno sky, the Towers is like a series of medieval openwork church spires, or the unclothed framework of aircraft fuselages made of decorated concrete. Such radical contrasts of images suggested by Rodia's architecture are revealing. Ancient iconographic shapes printed in their maker's mind from the southern Italian hill town landscape where he was born and spent his childhood are here translated into the technical verve and virtuosity of his new land, America.

The story of Sabato (Sam) Rodia's life cannot be separated from the story of his extraordinary construction. Without the Towers, his sufferings make no sense. With it, every gasp of his struggle to survive and rise above his disappointments becomes a breath of genius.

Rodia, an Italian immigrant construction worker, put 30 years of his life into building the spires that rise above the little houses of Watts. "I had in my mind to do something big and I did," is how he summed up the decades of intensive work and sacrifice that went into making the Towers.

There have been many myths, misconceptions and mistakes in the versions of Rodia's life that have gained currency since the mid-1920s, when he began to build his Towers. Since 1954, when Rodia walked away from his completed masterpiece, never to see it again before his death in Martinez, northern California, in 1965, the confusion has intensified. This account is as close to Sam Rodia's true story as it is possible to verify:

Sabato Rodia was born in the village of Rivotoli near the town of Nola in the province of Campania in southern Italy. Naples, the capital of Campania, is about 20 miles to the west. No record of Rodia's exact birth date has been found, but his gravestone in Martinez, put there by his family, is inscribed with the legend: "Sam Rodia: 1875-1965."

The Rodias of Rivotoli were landed peasantry in a region that had changed little since medieval times until the 19th century. Nola, favored by the emperors of Rome and by later Norman and Aragonese conquerors, is a town rich in decaying castles, palaces and villas decorated with old mosaics. After the unification of the Kingdom of Italy in 1861, the north rapidly industrialized. The south, or Mezzogiorno, had its ancient medieval way of life disrupted first by Napoleonic land reforms and the shift from a pastoral to an agricultural economy with the conversion of forests and meadows to farm fields, and by a harsh exploitation by northern interests.

For a bright young southern boy without education, emigration was the main escape from a probable future of hard farm labor, harsh taxation, malaria and the millitary draft at age fifteen. Sabato (or Sabatino in the diminutive) was named for the sabbath because he was intended for the priesthood. Service to the Roman Catholic church was a tradition in the extended Rodia family, which boasts several bishops in its lineage.

But the young Sabatino, his niece Angie Alexander remembers older family members saying, was "a natural anarchist." The teenage boy who followed his older brothers to America some time in the late 1880s or early 1880s bore a soul grown in a native soil enriched by Etruscan, Greek, Roman, Norman, Arab, Spanish and French layers of fertile cultural reference. These resonances vibrate in the southern Italian air, in the imagery every child sees in his village, his church, his local pageantry, his daily life.

It is possible, according to most family remembrance, that Sabato Rodia never learned to read or write, either in his native Italian, in the English of his new homeland, or in the Spanish of his later Los Angeles barrio. On a social security application he filed in the 1930s he had to repeat the letters of his name several times on the edge of the paper before he could sign the form. Another social security application from 1937 displays Rodia's vagueness about his own date and place of birth, which is given as April 15, 1886 in Rome. On the same form he gives his mother the unlikely maiden name of "Rosen."

The Rodia brothers settled first in the Pennsylvania coalfields. Here one brother changed his name to Dick Sullivan, to find work in a tough region dominated by Irish union men wary of underpaid Italian "scabs." Sullivan was later killed in a mining explosion, a casualty of the Rodias' exchange of the Old World for the New.

Sabato became known as Sam at this time. He was the first Rodia to make his way to the West Coast, settling in Seattle, where, according to the only marriage certificate ever traced naming Sam Rodia, he married Lucy Ucci in 1902. Sam's first son was born in Seattle, but the next year the family moved to the town of Fruitvale, near Oakland. Sam brought his beloved sister Angelina, her husband Sam Colacurcio and their two children from Pittsburgh to join him in the Bay Area.

There, Rodia worked as a quarryman, in roadbuilding gangs and as a cement mason for the city of Oakland. After the 1906 earthquake he was employed as a construction laborer in San Francisco. He had no formal training as a tile-setter, as some legends claim.

The marriage to Lucy produced two sons, and a daughter who died in early childhood. Sam never settled into domesticity, and started drinking heavily. In 1909 Lucy, citing "general neglect," took her children and walked out on the "the drunken bum," as he had become known in the family. Rodia was so erratic that his wife could not even get his child support payments. In 1912 Sam and Lucy were formally divorced. Sam, by all accounts, never saw Lucy or his sons Alfred and Frank again.

To his brother-in-law Sam Colacurcia, Rodia remained a "gypsy" all his life. Colacurcio took the main immigrant highway to happiness in America; he worked hard as a blacksmith for an oil company, bought a home, fathered 17 children, and gathered honor and respect. To this good man Sam Rodia was a worthless renegade.

Rodia in his thirties was a roisterer and a boozer. After being abandoned by his wife and children, he disappeared for a decade. Many rumors persist about Rodia's whereabouts, fuelled by his own inventive storytelling. He may have gone to Mexico, to Texas or Wisconsin, or served with the Army in France during World War I.

This blank space in Rodia's history is crucial. He left Oakland a dedicated drinking man with no sign of ambition, artistic or otherwise; he reappeared as a sober worker with a vision haunting his dreams.

Rodia resurfaced publicly in 1918 in Long Beach, accompanied by a Mexican woman named Benita, who many have been his second wife. Benita Rodia is listed on records as co-tenant of the house they rented in Long Beach.

The South Bay area was popular with Italians, Greeks and Portuguese for its Mediterranean climate and coastline and its excellent fishing industry. In his Long Beach house, 1216 Euclid Avenue, Rodia, now a sober, steady wage earner, first tried out his artistic talents in tangible form. He made fountains and garden pergolas (and perhaps a carousel) in decorated reinforced concrete. These modest objects, which echo some of the structural and decorative elements Rodia used in his later masterwork in Watts, were demolished in 1961, along with the Euclid Avenue house.

Sam's intimate relationships weren't going well. Benita left him and a woman called Carmen, who later moved with Sam to Watts, cleaned him out and skipped town, according to local gossip.

This last disaster seems to have confirmed Sam's acceptance of the failure of his personal life. "After Carmen left," says Brad Byer, Rodia's great-nephew "Sam never had anything to do with women again. When he started work on the Towers, he took a bath once a month maybe, with an alcohol rub, not with water, which he considered dangerous. The hair on his arms was caked with dried cement and bits of glass. No woman in her right mind would have given him a second look."

"He was short and slight - and much stronger than he looked" writes journalist James Peck, who met Rodia in the early 1950s. "His face was longish and pasty-gray, a blurry sort of face. He had dark, rheumy eyes; short, sparse lashes. He wore a suit coat and pants that matched only in the sense that they were equally ancient and filthy; a work shirt buttoned at the collar; and a venerable fedora, sweat-stained, greasy, worn through at the front crease. I remember the way he held his hands, straight and unbent, as if their flexibility were impaired. His body movements were crablike, more likely to be lateral than forward, but swift and well planned.

"He spoke with a pronounced Mediterranean accent, not at all difficult to understand. He showed little hesitancy in word choice and expressed himself succinctly and clearly when he wanted to. He also mumbled a lot to himself, and if you listened carefully he would tell you things that way that he wouldn't give you in clear text. Sam met - nay, exceeded - the most rigorous criteria for eccentricity, but the more time I spent with him, the more convinced I became that he was pretty damn bright. He just wouldn't mess with an idea he didn't like."

July, 1948

"Some say he murdered his wife and that this (the Towers) is his penance," one neighbor told writer Selden Rodman in the early 1950s. There are tales of Rodia speeding around in a 1927 red Hudson roadster with a fire-engine siren, liquored to the eyeballs, until, pursued by the police, he buried the auto under a tower. This is unlikely, for by then Sam Rodia was fully absorbed in "doing something big" to lift his spirit above the confusions of conventional life.

Searching for a location for his visionary architectures, Rodia first bought a property in Compton, in 1921 according to tax records. But he would never use it, because he soon found his triangular site in Watts. Title to 1765-69 107th St. E. was transferred to Rodia in 1929. He probably entered a lease-to-buy agreement four or five years earlier.

The usual story is that Rodia moved to Watts in 1921. The dates 1921 and 1923 are embedded in tile in the Towers. But is is more likely that he actually took up residence in the little clapboard cottage wedged beside the Southern Pacific railroad tracks some time between 1924 and 1927.

Back then, Watts was a sleepy urban village edged with onion fields and swampland in the trough of the Los Angeles basin. Annexed to the city of Los Angeles in 1926, its population was balanced between Anglos, Latinos and blacks with a few Japanese truck gardeners on the outskirts. The district was fairly peaceful and friendly, filled with little bungalows on small lots that had space for a few backyard goats, pigs and chickens. It was just the place for a private man to fit in and follow his own dream.

Throughout the late 1920s, '30s and '40s Sam Rodia worked on his Towers. At night, on weekends, in all weathers, every moment he could spare from his regular job as a construction worker, Rodia raised his remarkable architectures of spires, gazebos and fountains within a decorated wall with only three gates, and created the world of a miniature city carved out of the Watts flatland. He built himself a complete little town with its own streets, squares and spires, its tiny piazzas and cooling fountains, its sun patterns and its shadows. The images Rodia gave concrete form were a recollection of an older, deeper, richer more resonant world expressed in the technical virtuosity of modern America.

The Towers' decoration was pure Americana. The green 7-UP and blue Milk of Magnesia bottles Rodia collected in his sack as he wandered down the Southern Pacific tracks were mixed with decorative inserts of pottery, crockery and tile he chose carefully to give brilliant sparkle to his cement structures. As his towers rose, the diminutive Rodia clung to them with, some say, a window-washer's belt; or, as one old photo shows, Rodia bent iron rods around his waist and hooked them to the tower rungs. A burlap pouch filled with bits of glass, tile and seashells and a pail of wet cement complemented his simple tools: hammer, pliers, pincers. Enrico Caruso blaring from an old horn gramophone was his only companion during most of these long hours of labor.

When Rodia was in a sociable mood he would pay the local kids pennies and cookies for scraps of tile and bits of broken plate. One boy who grew up in the neighborhood while Rodia was building "Nuestro Pueblo" recalled that "Everybody said he was crazy, but I remember him up in the towers singing away." "He always kept the doors to his place locked," says another neighbor. "But he liked me well enough, and gave me permission to give my kids parties inside the towers. But nobody got to see in his house, ever."

"We ran over to him one day when the earth to began to shake," another neighbor reportedly said, speaking of the 1933 Long Beach quake in a 1967 article by Robert S. Bryan, "Sam Rodia and the Children of Watts." "That crazy guy was up there in his towers and the earth was shaking and we told him to come right down. But he just laughed. 'It won't fall', he said, and by gosh he was right!"

Rodia always worked alone. Queried about this in the early 1950s he said, "I had no help. I couldn't tell no one what to do because a millions times I didn't know what to do myself." Shown a photo of the massive Holy Family Catherdral in Barcelona, Spain, by the Catalan architect Antonio Gaudi, that some commentators have compared to the Watts Towers, Rodia asked: "Did this man have help?"

In the 1930s Rodia, long an enemy of any established faith, acted as an evangelist at the tent revival meetings of a Mexican group called The Cry of Christian Freedom. Rodia's favorite sermon, old handbills bearing his name show, was "True Freedom: Freedom of Spirit and Soul." A trough in the north wall of the Towers was probably used as a baptismal font during this period.

Obsessed by his growing Towers, Rodia neglected to wash or even to eat regularly. Angie Alexander, Rodia's niece, who lived in Los Angeles from 1935 to 1950 brought the busy builder food and mended his tattered clothes. "He lived a godawful life," she says. Sam's brother Tony, a building contractor who lived in Corona in Riverside County and was reputed to be a self-educated "scholar," dropped by only once to see his "bum brother."

Sarah Davis, a neighbor who still lives across 107th St. from the Towers, asked Rodia over for "hot biscuits and jelly. He enjoyed himself and was very friendly with the neighbors and all. He was like a squirrel up there. I was so afraid he was going to fall, but he never did."

"I asked him what the Towers cost him," says her husband Jack. "He told me the big one there in the middle cost him more than $3,000 in cement alone. He bought lots of 20-cent, 94 lb. bags of Portland cement. He had stone in there that cost him $40 a ton. He put all he had into those things, but he was a friendly man."

"One week I buy cement next week buy iron," Rodia said on a tape recorded late in his working life. "Every week use up all my money, buy things to keep working, keep working." This was the litany of Rodia's life for 30 hard years.

In the 1940s Sam Rodia's mood altered as Watts and the world around it changed. During World War II thousands of Southerners were drawn to Los Angeles to work in the war factories. In a racist city, Watts was the one gate of entry for blacks. The Anglos and Hispanics retreated from Watts, the Japanese market gardeners were interned as "enemy aliens." Watts became a black ghetto.

"Sam didn't relate to the new conditions," says Brad Byer. "In the Depression there were a lot of crusty old geezers like Sam around, and everyone was poor, and he felt part of things. When the wartime boom hit L.A., the old anarchist in Sam hated all the rampant materialism he saw around. He felt the world's values were going to hell" The Los Angeles region became industrialized. Modern America, with all its tense energies and restlessness, caught up with Sam Rodia.

He would rant about "painted whores in high heels," about "terrible income taxes," about the "oppressed classes and minorities of the world." He talked about "the poor fighting rich men's wars." He complained about "greed ruining the family and undermining basic values." Conjuring up his gallery of historic heroes - Galileo, Columbus, Alexander the Great, Marconi, Buffalo Bill, Amerigo Vespucci, Julius Caesar and Marco Polo - backed up by old volumes of the Encyclopedia Britannica he kept on his shelf but probably couldn't read, Rodia grew increasingly angry with the world. At times, according to some accounts, he identified his own predicament as a prophet without honor with the fate of Giordano Bruno, the Renaissance mystic born in Nola and burnt by the Church for heresy, or with St. Sebastian martyred by heathen arrows.

Musician Johnny Otis, who has organized the Watts Jazz Festivals, remembers his first encounter with this surly Rodia in the late 1940s. "I ran the Barrelhouse Club on Central Ave. and had a chicken ranch, The Progressive Poultry Co. of Watts, near the Towers. Yet I didn't really dig the Towers at first, or register their beauty. When I did it came upon me that this crazy old Italian man was some kind of amazing genius. So one day when I went up, knocked on the gate, asked to see over his place. He cussed me out and slammed the door in my face! The privilege of genius, I guess," Otis chuckles indulgently.

During World War II Rodia was made to observe the blackouts by taking down the lights that lit up his Towers. Rumors went around that the Towers were radio masts for the Japanese propagandist Tokyo Rose. Sam quarrelled with his patriotic neighbors, and the children of the new black settlers in Watts took the cue to scramble over the walls of the "Nuestro Pueblo" and dump garbage or smash the crockery embedded in the cement.

Approaching 80, Rodia was exhausted. He was then a small, tough, wiry old fellow barely five feet tall with a stubbled, big-nosed face hidden by a sweat-stained fedora. His huge hands were hard as hide, with muscles ribbing even the fingers. He could startle friends with a brilliant gaptoothed grin that opened up the warm brown eyes to reveal a profound tenderness.

Yet Sam was growing increasingly solitary and less able to make ordinary daily human contact. According to a story from his late period, Rodia's cottage was stacked with unopened packages of soap, even though he seldom bathed. It seems Sam bought single bars of soap to make change at the familiar corner shop so he wouldn't need to confront strange bus drivers on his journeys to work.

The Towers first received press attention in an April 28, 1937, Los Angeles Times item, luridly headlined "Glass Towers and Demon Rum." This piece is the source of much misinformation about Rodia, who was here sloppily tagged "Simon Rodilla." The false

"Simon" has stuck, and is now enshrined in the city's on-site plaque.

By the late 1940s Rodia had completed his vision. For the next five or six years he tinkered with the Towers, repairing damage, adding details here and there.

It is said he fell ill for three days alone in his house, perhaps with a stroke that presaged the heart failure that would eventually kill him. Once recovered, he decided to join his family in northern California and live out his life close to their care. One day in 1954 Sam Rodia gave his Towers away to a poor neighbor, and gave his goods and chattels away to anyone who happened to be around at the time. He never saw the Towers again, even though he lived for another 11 years.

When later asked what he wanted done with the Towers, Rodia reportedly said, "Just tell them to do whatever they please."

Rodia seemed not to care that his life's work was being vandalized by neighborhood kids and abused by hooligans who thought cash was hidden under some of the embedded plates. A year after Rodia left Watts his house burned down, leaving only a gateway, hearth, mirrored entry portico and tiled steps in a blackened ruin.

Rodia went to Martinez, a small city north of Berkeley where the main body of the Rodia-Colacurcio clan had settled. Sam had not seen most of his relatives in 45 years, but for a month-long visit in the late 1930s when he built his sister Angelina Colacurcia some garden ornaments that still exist.

He turned up at the Martinez bus station with a couple of suitcases and a bundle, and $10,000 sewn into the lining of his jacket, according to family recollection. Sam was independent to the end; he never wanted to need anybody. Despite his nest-egg, he lived frugally on social security benefits and refused all handouts.

Sam Colacurcio, the family patriarch, accepted the errant "gypsy" back into the fold with grudging grace. Rodia's sons Alfred and Frank, now middle-aged men, wanted nothing to do with their faithless father.

Rodia soon settled into an amiable routine. In the morning he left his Spartan rented room to sit on a bench by the railyard in the sunshine, or perch on the porch of Frank Colacurcio's butcher shop chatting to his cronies. Sometimes he helped out in his nephew's butchery or visited his niece Mary Lou Byer.

"He's no damn good," Sam Colacurcio said unrelentingly to writer Calvin Trillin who in 1964 was researching an article on Rodia for the New Yorker. "He's been an anarchist all his life. He used to sing anti-church songs with that drunken gang and make his sister (Angelina Colacurcio) cry."

1950

In 1959, when Rodia had been five years in sleepy Martinez, his Towers suddenly came to world attention. Provoked by an attempt by the Los Angeles City Building and Safety Department to demolish the Towers as "an unauthorized public hazard," an international outcry occurred.

Famous architects, artists and cultural pundits pronounced the towers a rare work of intuitive artistic genius. Buckminster Fuller declared that "Sam will rank with the sculptors of all history as time goes on. He is an artist with beautiful structural sense." Pilgrims beat a path to Rodia's door when he was located in Martinez, after a surprise appearance at a 1961 conference on the Towers at UC Berkeley. "We approached Sam with awe," says Jeanne Morgan, a founding member of the 1959 committee organized to take over the Towers and rally support for their preservation and maintenance.

What mattered most to Rodia at the end of his days was the new respect of many of his relatives, friends and neighbors in Martinez. Perhaps only his nephew Nick Calicura (a simplification of of Colacurcio) had any real notion of Rodia's achievement, but the late sunshine of the family's attention warmed the dusk of the old man's life.

Rodia's last six months were spent in a nursing home after a heart attack. He fiercely resented being put among "dying people" and tried to run away several times, till he had to be tied to his bed. He was lucid and wiry to the end, a tough 90-year-old who, visitors remember "had a big smile on his face."

On July 25, 1965 Sabato Rodia surely died happy, knowing that, like his historical heroes, he had accomplished greatness. His sons Alfred and Frank attended the funeral. A small granite block marks his grave in the Martinez cemetery.

These sentences from a 1978 letter to Mayor Tom Bradley by Sir Kenneth Clark could serve as Rodia's memorial. "Apart from their intrinsic beauty, they (the Towers) represent a marvellous piece of self-sacrifice and devotion which was characteristic of the early immigrants...I would like once more to say what an important part they play in the world's estimate of Los Angeles."

Maybe Rodia's own simple statement should be his epitaph: "I had in mind to do something big and I did."

Sam Rodia's Towers in Watts is the work of a natural artist-architect who imagined it as a visionary whole. The structural concept and the decorative patterns are a unity. A powerful symbolic imagination is at work, capable of grand schemes. Though Rodia amended and experimented as he went along, changing and refining as any artist would do in a labor 30 years long, there is no sense that he fumbled in the dark. The central idea was always in his mind, whatever moments of doubt and indecision he may have had along the way. The finished work has the structural sophistication, technical certainty and conceptual force of a major art work.

If you examine the way this architecture was made, you must set aside any notion of classifying it as "folk art."

What we conventionally and somewhat condescendingly consider folk art usually starts small, then adds and elaborates, expanding by makeshift and fortunate accident. The folk artist unlike the professional artist, is not trained to think in terms of a total composition executed by a formal procedure. The charm of folk art lies in its touching tentativeness and artless naivete.

"To dismiss this unique creation as a quaint folly, as one more bizarre production of an eccentric folk artist, would be an error," William Seitz of New York's Museum of Modern Art wrote of the Towers in his book The Art of Assemblage. "Rodia's Towers is much more than uncontrolled accretions of junk. His innate artistry is evident everywhere in masterful contrasts and analogies of sizes and textures, man-made and natural materials, organic and geometric forms, monochromatic and complementary color schemes, and opacity and transparency...These elements are all harmonized with the total structure. The Watts Towers is a unique creation of inspiring power and beauty."

The Towers sprang whole out of Sam Rodia's heart and soul. It moves us not by its "primitive" charm, but by the power and grandeur of its conception and execution.

Buckminster Fuller, the visionary engineer-designer, had no doubt of this. Hardly a modest man, he ranked Rodia on a par with himself as a "natural engineering sculptor" who was free of the prejudices of any formal training.

"Rodia was a master of his material," Fuller said a long interview in March 1983, filmed shortly before he died. "He thought structurally, he thought powerfully. He thought in terms of nature producing a palm tree. How can that great palm be up there waving in the wind and not break down?"

Explaining Rodia's "very powerful sense of tension and compression," Fuller described the basic geometries that give the spires their slender strength. He demonstrated how Rodia's sculptural architecture is the most economic structural configuration.

These triangles are developed into four-sided tetrahedrons, eight-sided octahedrons and 20-sided icosahedrons, which Fuller notes are the "only three structural systems in the universe. All crystals, all biology are made up from these. The tetrahedron, for instance, has three triangles around each corner. Sam was really a pioneer thinker, daring to do his own thinking and feeling, using all three basic forms time and again. He had a real sense of how nature builds things."

Fuller added with great emphasis: "Sam was inspired by the very big question of reaching for the sky. He talked in only one language, which was that of a great engineering sculptor. In the presence of Sam Rodia's Towers, people who are intuitive feel the artist's powerful intuition of how nature really does things, how to do the most with the least, how to say the incredible amount that he did with so very little."

Rodia built his towers well. He rested them on shallow rocker foundations made of steel rails, pipes and angle irons set in concrete to allow the spires to sway with seismic shocks. The towers, still half-built, survived the 1933 Long Beach major quake without damage, though the tremors cracked the foundation of City Hall 10 miles further from the temblor's epicenter.

To link the Towers' shafts, ribs and spokes Rodia spliced and lapped iron angles and tees and wrapped them with expanded metal mesh and chicken wire, which he then handpacked with cement. He used no bolts, welds or rivets. This simple junction, now known as the Rodia Joint, foreshadowed the thin-shelled concrete structures of the great Italian architect-engineer Luigi Nervi who, in the 1950s and '60s, designed vast Olympic stadiums in Rome in ferro-cement.

Nervi was a highly trained and experienced engineer. Rodia was an unskilled construction worker. Therein lies the measure of the man's invention.

Rodia worked without scaffolding, with nothing but a pail of cement hung over one arm and a bag for tools, mainly a hammer, pincers and pliers, tied around his waist. He was a small man, barely five feet tall, and the reach of his arms determined the natural rhythm of his structure's ribs and struts. He stood on one rib to work on the next above, anchored to one of the shafts with a window-washer's belt or a steel rod bent around his waist. He toiled night and day, on weekends, come rain or shine.

The sequence of the Towers' construction is not reliably documented. Rodia drew no plans and made no sketches; it was all in his head. "Sometimes I don't know myself what to do" he once said. It is thought that he built the enclosing wall first, then the twin-masted "ship" tucked into the prow of the triangle. Rodia's nephew Nick Calicura visited the Towers in the 1930s and claims to remember that the center and the eastern towers had been built by then, but the western had not.

This sequence seems to be confirmed by the increasing structural economy shown in the three tall spires, moving east to west. The 57-foot east tower has a fat core like a pile of fountain bowls propped by thickish ribs. The central tower, at 96 feet 10 inches, has a double ring of legs in an excess of supports, but is still considerably leaner than its eastern neighbor. The west tower, 99-and-a-half feet tall, rests lightly on sixteen slender shafts spaced about the perimeter to distribute the natural maximum load lines. Its central spine is thin and its ribs are lean.

Creator of the Watts Towers, Sam Rodia. W.T.H., 1960

The decorative elements emphasize the Towers' structural patterns. None of the decoration is haphazard "junk," as some visitors have described it. Rodia chose carefully, using colorful mosaics, seashells, pottery, crockery, colored glass and tile slips to add sparkle to the tower ribs all the way to the top. Green 7-UP bottle bottoms and blue Milk of Magnesia glass are given new life as impromptu murals. Terracotta inserts, Ernest Batchelder and Malibu tiles, plates and dishes from the extinct Vernon and Bauer pottery works make the Towers a veritable museum of the lost glory of southern California art pottery in the 1920s and '30s.

Rodia could be baroque when he wanted. The entrance canopy to his now burnt-out cottage on the edge of the Towers has a ceiling set with mirrors and little pottery zebras, unicorns and elephants. The red and beige cement flooring is inscribed with patterns of hearts and flowers.

There are witty details everywhere: a Winged Victory on a spire peak, teapot spouts sticking out of walls, a cowboy boot and a cement foot, corncobs pressed into concrete, rosette patterns made from pressing a faucet handle into wet cement, impressions of work tools, horseshoes and starfish patterns drawn in concrete or encrusted with mosaic.

"Cactus gardens" of cement succulents sparkling with shards of colored glass spring out of the walls. A birdbath and baptismal font are brilliant with inset tile. The thin-masted "Ship of Marco Polo" at the prow of the site is encrusted with white seashells that give its contours the rich texture of carved marble.

Jules Langsner, who wrote the first serious article on the Towers in the July 1951 issue of Arts & Architecture, recalled that Rodia "was completely indifferent to his appearance. I remember going out there one summer, and he had on an old shirt cut off at the shoulders, and his arms were just covered with bits of glass, dust from the chipping, all embedded in his arms as they were in the towers. It would have taken weeks of steam baths and scrubbing with wire brushes to start to get it off."

But, as Langsner adds, "Rodia didn't seem to notice. He lived in a self-enclosed world, and he had a fantastic obsession - a monument. He wanted to be remembered."

In a 1952 film made by William Hale, then a film student at USC, Rodia is shown scavenging the railroad track beds for fragments of glass or bending his iron rods by hand under the rails, or poring over the workbench loaded with orderly piles of pottery and tile. You get glimpses of the inside of his cottage, which burnt down in 1955, the year after he walked away from his Towers forever. The interior of Rodia's house is sparse, the furnishings minimal. The tiled fireplace, which still stands, a row of soiled Encyclopedia Britannicas, and an old horn gramophone are the only luxuries.

Dr. Joseph Bronowski writes in his book The Ascent of Man that the Towers are "one of my favorite monuments..." which "in the 20th century take us back to the simple, happy and fundamental skill from which all our knowledge of the laws of mechanics grows."

What were the images Sam Rodia carried in his head? What iconography did he bring with him out of his childhood?

Rodia's great-nephew Brad Byer believes that "Sam's artistic imagery was inspired by what he saw in his childhood in the hill village, by the cathedral spires of Naples and, in the neighboring town of Nola, by the great Roman mosaics, the ruined castles and palaces; and the ceremonial towers of wood and ribbons, sometimes 50 feet high, carried in the Festa de Gigli (Festival of Lilies) celebrating San Gennaro, Nola's patron saint."

Others have compared Rodia's Towers to the "Dream Palace" of the French mailman Ferdinand Cheval constructed in the town of Hauterives from 1879 to 1921. But Cheval's quirky structures show none of the engineering genius of the Towers. The golden stupas of Siam, Russian Constructivist sculptures, the junk collages of the 1920s German Bauhaus artist Kurt Schwitters have also been mentioned as possible comparisons or inspirations.

But Rodia, an untutored laborer, had no access to such precedents. His only store of images was the one he carried around in his head, accumulated through his Campania childhood and his adult working life in America. This reservoir, and the man's own original imagination, are the true sources of his creation.

Byer says without hesitation that "Sam's motive energy was a spiritual force." He relates a story of his great-uncle at the famous conference on the Towers at UC Berkeley in 1961, when Rodia was first introduced to a crowd of his admirers." A professor kept pestering Sam with questions about the significance of the many heart designs in the Towers. Rodia ignored him; finally irritated, he pointed to a young couple cuddling nearby and said, 'Ask them!'

Byer believes that "a unique set of circumstances came together in the Towers. Sam came out of an Italian master builder tradition, out of a medieval society that hasn't really changed in 2,000 years. Then he suffered the scorn Italian immigrants had to endure in California in the early part of the century. Without formal education in general, and art training in particular, his deeply religious imagination was free to dream up its very own shapes."

"One begins to realise how old the real Italy is," D.H. Lawrence writes in 'Sea and Sardinia.' "Here since endless centuries man has tamed the impossible mountainside into terraces, he has quarried the rock... Wherever one is in Italy, either one is conscious of the present, or of the medieval influences, or of the far mysterious gods of the early Mediterranean... The land has been humanized through and through."

"The whole village with its compact, hard-edged form symbolized a man-centered world," architect-photographer Norman Carver writes in his book Italian Hilltowns, "a place where man appeared to control his destiny, no matter how tenuously, in the midst of an often hostile environment."

Another possible native image Rodia might well have brought with him from southern Italy is that of the *trulli*. These conical stone-roofed dwellings or storehouses "dot the almond and olive groves of southern Apulia," writes Bernard Rudofsky in his book Architecture Without Architects. "They are built of annular stone rings that terminate in a false conic cupola crowned by a keystone. The archaic house form of an early megalithic civilization...the type has survived almost without change since the second millennium B.C."

Whole *trulli* towns, like Alberobello, still survive in the southern Italian landscape. In silhouette these clusters of cones resemble a squat version of the Watts Towers. In neighboring Sardinia

the similar stone *nuraghi* are elongated versions of *trulli* similar in profile to Rodia's spires.

In the end, however, any truly original work of art or architecture is its own true provenance. Whatever the conscious or unconscious models that may have molded the mind of such a creator, the work itself is its own genesis, a unique artifact inventing its own origins.

The trullo, an ancient house design common in the southern Italian region of Sam Rodia's birthplace, may have been a source of his inspiration for the Watts Tower.

The literal history of Rodia's Towers since the creator walked away from his creation in 1954 is a murky tale.

Rodia gave the Towers to a poor neighbor, Louis Sauceda, who in turn sold them to Louis Montoya, a dairy worker, for $1,000. Montoya had dreams of turning the Towers into a taco stand, but instead he sold them for $3,000 in 1959 to two young Towers enthusiasts, Nick King and Bill Cartwright.

In the five years after Rodia departed, the Towers was vandalized by children looking for the treasure rumored to have been hidden by the "crazy old Italian." Decorative plates were smashed and garbage was dumped over the walls. In 1957 city officials issued a demolition order.

A battle began between the city and a newly formed Committee for Simon Rodia's Towers in Watts. In 1959, the Los Angeles City Department of Building and Safety, which had condemned the Towers as "an unauthorized public hazard," agreed to a stress test devised by N.J. "Bud" Goldstone, Senior Test Engineer with the Engineering Development Laboratory at North American Aviation (now Rockwell International Corp.).

Bud Goldstone devised an ingenious load test to determine the Towers' resistance to wind pressure, which was the city engineers' main concern. Goldstone had done a stress analysis on the structural safety of the Towers, but was compelled by the bureaucrats to conduct a load test to prove his point in practice.

In a 1963 article in Experimental Mechanics titled "Structural Test of a Hand-Built Tower," Goldstone described how he chose to place stress on the tallest, western tower with a 10,000 lb. critical load. 'If one sample tower...withstood the required wind-load simulation for five minutes without collapsing, then all of the structures would be declared safe."

Pressure was applied in 1,000 lb. increments and readings were taken at each stage of the increase. "The final run to 10,000 lb. was terminated after one minute," Goldstone wrote, "when the 10-inch WF (wide-flange) beam began yielding. This time for load application, although shorter than the five minutes specified, was satisfactory to the representative of the Building and Safety Department."

In other words, the testing apparatus failed way before the tower showed any sign of strain.

No cement cracked during the test. The maximum deflection, 1 5/8-inches at 70 feet, was well within acceptable limits. But Goldstone was sweating.

"Attempting the stress analysis on the Towers was a powerful professional challenge," he says now. "And I've worked on the Apollo moonshot program and the lunar landing gear. Colleagues I approached at the time to check my calcs asked me why I was sticking my neck out for this odd enterprise. I had no clear answer then, and still, after 25 years of devotion to the Towers, I don't understand what got to me back then - but it was powerful!"

The fact that the Towers had to be subjected to such drastic, and possibly damaging testing is an instance of the city's often crass indifference to the Towers over the years. Art historian Kate Steinitz denounced the load test as "a barbaric measure comparable to a witch trial in the Middle Ages." Harold Manley, head of Building and Safety at the time of the test, wrote in the 1959 memo, "Personally, I think this is the biggest pile of junk outside a junkyard that I have ever seen." For the next 16 years the volunteer committee maintained the Towers, raised funds for its repair, built the neighboring Watts Towers Art Center after the 1965 Watts riots and in 1963 had the Towers listed as an historic monument by the Los Angeles Cultural Heritage Board and the National Register of Historic Places.

Goldstone reported that "long cracks, some more then five feet, with gaps measuring from 1/8 to 1/4-inch, were seen in ten or more vertical legs of the three tall towers. The situation is particularly serious since the tall tower legs get their strengths from the combination of cement cover and steel reinforcement...An immediate danger to the Towers exists, namely that loads caused by wind or seismic forces may buckle the tower legs which have been weakened by the loss of the continuity of their cement coverings."

In 1975 the Committee donated the Towers to the City of Los Angeles, which undertook to carry out necessary repairs and maintenance. The city's Public Works commissioner Waren Hollier gave the contract for this work to architect Ralph A. Vaughn.

This was a disaster. In 1978 the Committee for Simon Rodia's Towers in Watts, which retained residual rights of supervision over future programs of repair and restoration, invoked these rights in a lawsuit.

The Committee accused Vaughn and Hollier of botching the repairs and misusing state funds meant for the Towers. After a bitter fight the work was stopped and the Committee initiated a lawsuit with the Center For Law In The Public Interest suing the city for damages.

In May 1979 the Towers were deeded to the state of California, to carry out emergency repairs. This transfer of title made the Towers eligible for an appropriation administered by the state's Department of Parks and Recreation. The state passed Assembly Bill 990 in 1980, that earmarked a further $1,000,000 for the Towers' repair, and commissioned The Ehrenkrantz Group of San Francisco, to carry out a study of the Towers' requirements for long-term preservation and restoration.

The state's $1,200,000 repair program was concluded in September, 1985. The city is now responsible for the operation and maintenance of the Towers.

Zdravko Barov, Conservator of Antiquities for the J. Paul Getty Trust, consulted by the state Dept. of Parks and Recreation in 1978, quoted Article 12 of the charter of conservation from the International Congress of Architects and Technicians of Monuments: "The elements used to replace missing parts should be harmoniously integrated with the original, but they should also be distinguishable from the original because the restoration should not imitate the monument either in its artistic appearance or its historical aspect."

The 1983 Towers Maintenance and Restoration Guide prepared by The Ehrenkrantz Group makes this crucial point: "It is essential that all involved in both maintenance and restoration appreci-

Sam Rodia with wire hangers arranged to form a tower profile.

ate, as Simon (sic) Rodia did, that the Towers will never be complete or entirely stable. There will be a permanent need for inspection and repair following and during the present catching-up period of major repair. 'Little and often' is the most cost-effective and satisfactory approach to extending the longevity of the monument, once the major structural repairs are completed."

The work of the State Architect's Office strengthened the Towers structurally by bolting damaged joints with stainless steel. It replaced with blank mortar those decorated cement areas that have deteriorated. However, as architect Andrew Rabeneck of The Ehrenkrantz Group insisted, "The Towers need constant ongoing love and care. It's a materially volatile art work out in the open, subject to all weathers, and to its own decay."

IV

WATTS
Leon
Whiteson

One major difficulty Watts has faced in the last forty years is its notoriety as a symbol as well as simply a place. This symbolic "Watts" is a bleak country of the mind that traps outsiders and insiders alike.

Watts is too often seen as an image of dark chaos haunting the American dream. It is the physical terror we might all suffer is we were poor, old or unprotected; it is the psychic fright of failure.

Mainstream America needs the notion of the ghetto. The stubbornly negative outside view of places like Watts is an indication of the intense emotional investment this nation has in the concept of the "ghetto," usually black or brown, as a clear-cut warning of failure in a society based on success. How may most of us measure our own "pursuit of happiness" except by contrast with these miseries?

The Rodia Towers in Watts and Watts itself have often shared the same fate in the city to which they belong. Both have suffered frequent neglect and stubborn indifference, relieved by spasmodic episodes of concern.

Sam Rodia's Towers is the masterpiece of a man who, humble in circumstance but not in spirit, found a way to show the world the magnificence of his soul.

The Towers is a strong symbol for the people who live around it. It is a beacon signalling one man's triumphs over a hostile host society in a metropolis still unsympathetic to the people of Watts, and to many of the city's poor new immigrants. Sam Rodia's visionary architecture beckons its neighbors to take heart - no matter how often they are snubbed or rejected by the rest of Los Angeles, and by America at large.

During the August 1965 disturbances in Watts, that outsiders call a riot and Wattsians call a revolt, the Rodia Towers was unscathed. A few hundred yards up the road 103rd St. was "Charcoal Alley" where fires blazed and thousands of police and National Guardsmen erected barricades to control the nightmarish carnival gaiety of those six hot days and nights that cost 34 lives, 1,000 injuries, 4,000 arrests and $40,000,000 in property damage.

"The Watts Towers is an important symbol to us of creative endeavour against all odds," says John Outterbridge, director of the Watts Towers Arts Center located beside the Towers. "It stands as a monument to a man who found a way of showing the whole world what he was made of. Under the rough skin of the uneducated Italian immigrant construction worker, Sam Rodia was a giant of a man. The Towers symbolizes that giants can walk out of this neighborhood called Watts."

"Wherever I travel, in the U.S. or abroad, and people hear my district includes Watts," says 15th District Councilwoman Joan Milke Flores, "I hear the response: 'Oh, you mean the riots?' What I try to express is that Watts is a community, not a riot."

The area around Rodia's Towers is a microcosm of Watts. It is a patchwork of small bungalows on 25-foot lots with chickens in the back yard, fenced off wasteland, decaying railroad tracks, a new housing development named Rodia Homes, churches and vest-pocket parks. Middle-aged winos woozy on cheap rotgut watch the youngsters pouring out of Markham Junior High School beyond the Watts Station.

When Sam Rodia bought his triangular lot on 107th St. E. in the 1920s Watts was a sleepy urban village on the edge of downtown Los Angeles with a peacefully mixed population one third Anglo, one third Hispanic and one third black. Charles H. Watts, a Pasadena realtor, gave his name to the town, which was incorporated as a separate city in 1907.

Back in the 19th century, under Mexican rule, Watts and its surrounding region was given to Anastacio Abilo as one of the land grants which followed the secularization of the missions. El Rancho Tajuata, as it was known, lay in the trough of the Los Angeles basin. Cattle shared the swamps and fields of mustard weed with sheep, until the breakup of the California ranchos in the 1870s replaced ranchers with farmers.

Stage coaches linking downtown L.A. with the port of San Pedro ran along the edge of Watts, as did the later Pacific Electric Red Cars in the first half of this century, to be supplanted in their turn by the Harbor Freeway. Land booms in the 1880s and early 1900s developed Tajuata, following the street patterns laid out by surveyors in the 1870s. Central Ave., for example, follows the western boundary of the old rancho. The Los Angeles and San Pedro railroad, the first in L.A. County, followed the line of Alameda St. that has marked, since

1869, the eastern boundary of Watts, isolating it from neighboring white districts that were later often hostile.

The subdivision lots in Watts had 25-foot frontages laid out between narrow streets and long back alleys for horse-and-buggy stables. The lots sold for a dollar down and a dollar a week to attract young couples from the East, and also Mexican laborers employed by the rapidly expanding railroads. The Pacific Electric Watts Station was opened 1904.

Blacks first came to Watts in some numbers during World War I to work in the munitions factories, as a later and even more numerous generation was to do one world war later. "A spite deal sold the first land to the Negroes in the southern part of Watts," said a 1933 thesis by a USC sociologist. Some time around World War I the bottom half of Watts below 103rd St. became a Negro section known as Mudtown. The streets of Mudtown, which was like a transplanted slice of the Deep South, were "three or four wagon paths," Arna Bontemps wrote on her 1931 novel "God Sends Sunday." "In the moist grass along the edges cows were staked...Ducks were sleeping in the weeds, and there was in the air a suggestion of pigs and slime holes." Mudtown, then the sole district of black settlement in Los Angeles, was surrounded by white neighborhoods. In the 1920s the Ku Klux Klan, active in Compton to the south, almost seized control of the Watts city government. This political disturbance, and a need to link up with good water sources, induced Watts to seek annexation to the city of Los Angeles in 1926.

World War II changed Watts into an overwhelmingly black suburb. Once again war factories attracted thousands of poor Southerners to California. Between 1940 and 1965 the black population of L.A. County increased from 75,000 to 650,000. Anglos and Latinos moved away from Watts, upset by this huge black influx.

In the then racially segregated city of Los Angeles, Watts was the only gateway of entry for incoming blacks. In the 1980 census the population of the 15th District was 29,300, broken down into 25,000 blacks and 4,000 Latinos. In recent years numbers of Asians have settled in the area, and the proportion of Latinos has increased.

The older established black residents of Watts were also often upset by the flood of raw new Southern settlers. Many, along with those blacks who achieved some success in their new environment, moved out into more prosperous and less ghettoized districts to the west along Crenshaw Bvd. and West Adams Ave. Watts became, after the disturbances in August 1965, a symbol of urban violence whose shadow still clouds the judgement of outsiders.

"Watts is on its way back," said Mary Alice Maye, chairperson of the Watts Community Development Action Committee at the December 1984 opening ceremony of the new $12,000,000 Watts

Shopping Center on 103rd Street and Compton Ave., a few blocks north of the Rodia Towers. "On its way back as a place where people will want to come to shop, to visit, and yes, to live."

As Maye spoke a banner slung across 103rd St. proclaimed "I Love Watts."

The shopping center is an important facility in Watts. Part of the anger that fired the 1965 revolt was generated by the way poor people were charged more for groceries and other domestic essentials than the residents of the more affluent Westside. Lacking transport and time. Wattsians were captives of greedy shopkeepers.

The new Watts Shopping Center is a segment of a 107-acre Watts Redevelopment Project begun in 1969, funded by a $27 million subsidy from the U.S. Department of Housing and Urban Development. The center itself was subsidized by low interest loans to the developer by the city's Community Redevelopment Agency and by tax-exempt bond issues.

Mayor Tom Bradley, who was a "cop on the beat" in Watts in the early 1950s when Sam Rodia was completing his towers, lists the area's improvements in bricks and mortar. "Since 1965 we have built two health centers, six new housing developments with over 500 units the Martin Luther King Hospital, several senior citizens' centers, an L.A. County public service facility, the Westminster Neighborhood Association Center, and the new shopping center. I don't believe the circumstances today are anywhere near to what they were twenty years ago."

Still, the bare-bones statistics about Watts in the late 1980s are bleak. Some current facts:

More than one-third of all Watts families have incomes below the federal poverty level, up from one-fifth in 1970. Among children under six, half live in poverty.

70 percent of the births in Watts are to unmarried mothers. More than half of all Watts households are headed by a single parent, usually a woman. The black infant mortality rate in Watts is twice that of Westside whites. The death and illness rates in the area are the highest in Los Angeles County.

20 percent of fifth graders in Watts scored above average on reading achievement scores, compared to 48 percent citywide. In the 46-square-mile 1965 "riot curfew zone" there are now three times the number of people collecting welfare compared to 20 years ago.

Black unemployment, at 15 percent officially, is twice that of white. Among the black teenagers the official rate is 30 percent, but is probably closer to 50 or even 75 percent.

One-third of the residents live in old, crime-ridden public housing projects. All four of these massive projects - Nickerson Gardens, Jordan Downs, Imperial Courts, Hacienda Village - were built well before 1965. Many three-generation families have grown up in

An aerial view.

Nickerson Gardens, the city's largest public housing project, erected in 1955 as a halfway house to give needy families temporary homes while they got back on their feet. A number of residents are mothers by age 14, grandmothers by age 30. "Grow up, get pregnant, have baby, get an apartment" is the cycle of life for many young women in Watts today.

Los Angeles Police Dept. statistics show that twelve percent of the crimes committed in the Southeast Division occurred in or near Nickerson Gardens or Imperial Courts, which together house 7,000 residents. Street gangs make the fenced-off projects into private robber baron fields which even police officers enter only in force. In Watts the police are often seen, in the words of one senior officer as "an army of occupation."

"Watts is an obsolescent area in which all the social and physical weaknesses of urban living are to be found," states a 1947 report by the L.A. Dept. of City Planning.

A 1959 study by the South-Central Area Welfare Planning council says that "The continuous immigration of persons from different parts of the country makes it difficult to stabilize and stimulate long-term projects."

"When the rioting came to Los Angeles it was not a race riot in the usual sense. What happened was an explosion - a formless, quite senseless, all but hopeless violent protest engaged in by a few but bringing disaster to all," declared the 1965 McCone Commission.

"Conditions are as bad or worse in South-Central Los Angeles today as they were nineteen years ago...The basic problem is poverty, grinding, unending and debilitating for all whom it touches," states a 1984 report by the city and county Human Relations Commissions.

"Watts is worse than it was twenty years ago, in some ways," says Ted Watkins, director of the Watts Labor Community Action Committee, which has generated some extraordinary examples of self-help in the area. WLCAC was set up several months before the '65 revolt, and Watkins, a former United Auto Workers shop steward and long-time resident of Watts, has headed it ever since.

"There's much more dope and booze. One-parent families are now the rule around here. A generation has grown up since 1965 that has never worked, a whole new generation that's totally unskilled and unsocialized. These kids don't know what a job is all about because they have no expectation of ever being employed."

As for the proud new shopping center, Watkins says: "Only such highly subsidized projects can survive in Watts. The Lockheed Watts-Willowbrook plant set up in 1970, the Chevrolet Division factory set up by John DeLorean, the Watts Manufacturing Corp., the

Watts doll-making workshop, the 45-acre Watts Industrial Park on Imperial and Alameda have all faltered or failed. After the riots $150-200 million in federal funds were funneled into Watts, with pitiful results."

"The kids see all this depression and poverty all around them, and they get this attitude nothing's ever going to change," says a divorced mother of two who lives in the Jordan Downs Housing Project. "They just stop believing life can be any different."

A nineteen-year-old on a Watts street corner says with a shrug: "All the kids I grew up with are either locked up, crazy in the head, or dead. This place is the jungle, man, and there ain't no Tarzans."

Countering these glum dispatches from an urban war zone are the affirmative voices that add humanity to the undeniably hard facts about a district where 35,000 people work, play, create and live out their lives. This chorus of affirmation by insiders counters the negative reports on Watts by outsiders before, during and after the 1965 revolt.

Bill Coggins, executive administrator of the Kaiser Permanente Watts Counselling and Learning Center says his feelings about Watts today are "very upbeat. We have a number of resources to build upon now. We have new institutions. We still lack cultural and entertainment facilities like museums, movie theatres, galleries, even a good video parlor, none of which yet exist in Watts. We need help, but we've done a lot on our own."

Coggins grew up in New York's Harlem, which he says is "a million times worse than Watts ever was, or could be. In Harlem the visual and social deprivations are far more brutal."

Robert Saucedo, director of the Young People of Watts Improvement Center on Grape Street that runs after-school work programs for Watts gang members, who clean up the neighborhood by, among other things, painting out disfiguring graffiti, says: "Watts is nowhere near as dangerous as it was ten years back. I was born here and have lived here all my life, and I can see how the place looks and feels better all the time. In the Center we have 25 kids from the ages of ten to eighteen who come in voluntarily. We try to help them get ready for the proper jobs. It's a mixed bunch racially, half black, half Latino, and they all get along pretty good. Not all gang members are killers, you know."

"What these kids need most of all is positive reinforcement," says Paris Earl, an actor who runs a theatre workshop for Watts schoolchildren. "There's so much raw talent down here. Folks call this a ghetto, but Watts is more like a dynamo, in my experience. That creative energy just bubbles up like natural gas. It can light up the town or burn up the streets, depending on whether it's used or abused."

The late Birdell Chew-Moore, a graduate of Budd Schulberg's famed Watts Writers Workshop and one of the area's revered elder stateswomen, said emphatically: "I feel very positive about Watts. Things here changed so much for the better after Tom Bradley got to be mayor, but folks outside still want to keep up a lot of static about Watts, for their own sad reasons."

Freda Shaw Johnson, planning chairperson for the Watts Health Center, another admired Watts senior, adds her voice to the chorus of affirmation. "Everybody wants only to write about the ugly in Watts. Why don't people outside ever want to hear that there's lot of love here? Don't they see that a lot of our anger stems from having that love ignored, or flung back in our faces, returned with indifference or contempt?"

Balanced between the affirmation and the despair, between the love and the anger, between the encouragement and the desperation is the sense that "giants walk out of this neighborhood called Watts."

Budd Schulberg, who founded the Watts Writers Workshop on Long Beach St. in 1965 immediately after the disturbances, wrote in a 1979 Herald article that he "went down there (to Watts) to hear T-Bone Walker and other little known jazz greats in the honky-tonks of what was then a Southern enclave stitched to the outskirts of the crazy quilt that is Los Angeles."

Other great jazz and rhythm-and-blues musicians to come out of Watts include Charlie Mingus, Esther Phillips, Johnny Otis and Buddy Colette. Otis, who played the famous old Club Alabam' on Central Avenue before opening his own club, the Barrelhouse, says of Rodia that "he was doing in a grand way what I was doing in my little way. Charlie Mingus grew up here as a poet writing about Rodia, transposing this feeling into aspects of his music."

Schulberg said of Watts that "If instead of creative talent this was oil seeping through the ground and being wasted, I can hear the businessmen of America, the practical, business-minded community crying 'what a waste!' Imagination is going to waste. Even hostility can be turned into a positive force."

State Assemblywoman Maxine Waters, who represents Watts, and who lived through the violence of August 1965, said in 1980 that "Watts has new buildings, but there's still no jobs, and the transportation system is still lousy. The housing projects are packed with PCP - 'angel dust.' The police, who are still basically aggressive, believe that the only thing that keeps blacks from acting worse is to beat them on the head."

"Watts is a kind of U.S. Bantustan," says musician Babalade Olamina, who was baptised Sherman McKinney. "We are the dumping ground of white America, in symbol as well as fact. If you fail in this nation you're not only no good, you are bad. It's the trash heap of history for us, brother."

39

"I'm as terrified to visit Beverly Hills as many white people are to visit Watts," says Paris Earl. "Over there I have my friends escort me to my car to prevent the police jumping on my back soon as I show my black face in the street."

John Outterbridge is a painter who has run the Watts Towers Arts Center since 1976. The Center, working on a minimal budget, offers classes for children in music, photography, video, African dance, drama, painting and Black history, as well as mounting exhibitions of the work of local artists. Schools from all over the L.A. area pay visits to the Center.

"Our kids need to create to keep from screaming," Outterbridge says. "Black talents like Richard Pryor and Eddie Murphy show what I mean. Their comedy is sharpened by their anger. It's screaming turned into laughter."

Talking of a young Crips Gang member who attends a music workshop at the Center, Outterbridge emphasizes: "You have to respect young people, no matter what you think of their styles. These kids jump on anything good to do, to express their inner song. It takes a gutty cat to share his tune. It's all part of the belief that art has the power of prayer, that the Rodia Towers is a psalm to the greater glory of God and man."

This is what Sam Rodia's Towers means to Watts. It stands almost one hundred feet high above the little bungalows, the wasteland and the disused rail tracks that surround it as a brilliant beacon to every man, woman and child in Watts, in Los Angeles and in the world to take courage in his own dreams.

Contemporary America is a harder and more selfish place than it was in the reformist 1950s and '70s, and its "failures" cannot but respond to the temper of the times. Sam Rodia toiled for thirty years to "do something big," to rise above the frustrations of an illiterate immigrant. His sparkling spires poke up out of the social, geographic and spiritual flatlands of the trough of the Los Angeles basin as labors of an exceptional love.

For some it may seem a mockery that this masterpiece of visionary architecture is located in one of the city's poorest districts. Several Westside wits have suggested that the Rodia Towers be put on wheels and relocated on Wilshire Boulevard, where it would be in full view of mainstream L.A.

But the location of the Towers in Watts is no mockery or accident. The Towers is the work of a poor immigrant who found the resources in himself to show all the world who he really was in his heart. The Towers is a beacon of hope for all those who find it hard to make their way through the formal structures of success in contemporary America.

For Watts, the Towers serves as a potent symbol that the district is "not a riot but a community."

V

A Tour of the
Watts Towers

by Arloa Paquin-Goldstone
& N.J. Bud Goldstone

Welcome to the famous Watts Towers. The Towers is on the Registry of Historic Places of the National Trust of the United States and is a Cultural Heritage Monument of the City of Los Angeles.

People come from all over the world to see them every year.

All the sculptures you see were built by one man, Sabato "Sam" Rodia, an Italian-American laborer, during every spare moment each day after work on the weekends over a 30 year period from the mid-1920s to 1954. Sam was also known as Simon Rodilla, Simon Rodia, and Don Simon by some neighbors, visitors, or reporters.

The intricate towers and surrounding wall were built on the triangular lot which also held his house. The main vertical legs of the sculptures are slender columns containing internal steel reinforcements, tied with wire, wrapped with wire mesh, and covered by hand with mortar.

The objects and materials embedded in the mortar were all carefully selected from available sources, circa 1920 - 1950, and the artist's choices are excellent examples of these objects and materials which were popular household and decorative items of the time. Even though these items were quite common in many American households during their time of manufacture, they are now seen as important elements in the history of Califonia (and American) decorative arts of the first half of the 20th century. Many of these items can now be found in antique shops, galleries and even the permanent collections of several museums.

The materials used include glass, mirrors, seashells, rocks, ceramic tile, pottery, and marble. The glass, usually parts of beverage bottles, is predominantly green from 7-UP bottle pieces or blue from Milk of Magnesia. There are none that are clear, such as used in Coca Cola bottles of that era.

The tiles are of many types, with many from the Malibu Potteries in Malibu, California where the artist was employed. The firm was in business only from 1926 to 1932 and sold its wares through a showroom and warehouse on Larchmont Boulevard. Even though the firm was in business for only a few years, many tiles were produced and can still be found in homes and structures built in Southern California during the late 20's and early 30's. Malibu Potteries produced a full line of tile for almost every architectural purpose, either interior or exterior. The tiles are polychromatic and are "among the most beautiful finely detailed and well executed pieces of their kind manufactured locally" according to architectural historian Kathryn Smith. They can be distinguished by their reproduction of European hand decorated tiles known as Saracen or Moorish and are primarily abstract and geometric in design.

In addition to the Malibu tiles, the viewer will also find a few areas decorated with tiles from the Batchelder Tile Company. Even though there are fewer Batchelder wares to be found in the Towers, these tiles are as prominent in the history of the decorative arts in Southern California as are those of Malibu Potteries. (The lack of many Batchelder tiles in relation to the number of Malibu tiles found in the Towers gives some credence to statements made by former Malibu employees that Rodia worked there for a time and would go home on weekends with pockets and bags full of discards and broken pieces of tiles.)

The Batchelder Tile Company, later know as Batchelder - Wilson, and Gladding McBean and Co. was originally founded by Ernest A. Batchelder in 1909 in Pasadena. The early Batchelder tiles, those found in the front wall of the Towers, differ stylistically from the Malibu tiles in that they are of the Craftsman Movement and are of a softer, more somber pallette. However, the later Batchelder tiles did move from the Craftsman style into the Spanish Colonial and Precolumbian revivals and on into Art Deco. One of these earlier tiles, a Viking Ship in the lower front wall, can also be found in the permanent collection of the Smithsonian Institute.

In addition to the Batchelder and Malibu tiles, the largest Southern California tile company, Gladding, McBean and Company, is most likely represented in the Towers as well.

We are very fortunate today to have in the Towers a repository of elements produced in California during the early 20th Century when California styles, Craftsman and the Spanish Colonial Revival or Mediterranian in particular, produced such a diversity of decorative designs. The tiles and their manufacturers were even the subject of a government study published by the California State Mining Bureau in 1928. This report, The Clay Resources and the Ceramic Industry of California, states that "The artistic development of California Decorative tile is an outstanding contribution to ceramic art in the United States. There is perhaps no other region in the world today that produces such a wide diversity of wall and fireplace tile, or that is so well prepared to create new designs for private homes, hotels stores and office buildings."

That the Towers is so typically Southern California is due in large part to its decorative elements, many of which are products of Southern California's prominence and proliferation in the pottery and tile manufacturing industries of the first half of the 20th century. Just as Rodia brought art and technology together in the makeup of the towers, the tiles and wares found in them are also a rich history of the meshing of artistic influences and technological advances made in Southern California during the early and mid 20th Century.

Nowhere else was there such an abundance of the raw materials (high quality clays) and the economic climate of growth to stimulate an industry to make use of them as well as a great diversity of architectural design and decorative styles to create a taste for such items. And all Rodia had to do was walk the streets and alleys of Los Angeles to glean this treasured ephemera of our daily lives.

You are standing in front of the entrance to Sam Rodia's Towers and to his house, which was right behind the entrance.

On both sides of the entrance, there is a mailbox with Rodia's initials, "S R" and the street address, "1765 East 107th Street". Although Rodia probably received little if any mail and possibly couldn't read, he built the two mailboxes into the front wall next to his front entrance. Above the entrance, he put the address, again, and his initials, this time with a reversed "s".

Inside the entrance is the decorated facade of the front wall to the house. The house itself is gone, burned in 1955, a year after Rodia left, handing over the deed to his house and towers to a neighbor. All that remains of the house is the front facade, posts along what was the east wall of the house, and the fireplace and chimney.

The canopy over the entrance, between the outside wall and the house, contains rows of pottery objects unicorns, horses, dolls, and more placed in the cement.

Along the side of what was the east wall of the house, remain a series of decorated posts. This post contains some of the pieces of broken California pottery also used by Rodia for decorations throughout the sculptures.

Turning eastward from the front door of the house, you enter the patio with its decorated floor from which the sculptures rise. Immediately east of the entrance are two of the small towers.

To the north is the very intricate "Gazebo", with its 40 foot tall spire and inside seating circle. Sit down on the long circular bench and you can view and enjoy the two small sculptures to the south, the chimney to the west, the rear, north wall, and the tallest tower on the east. Rodia has placed a great assortment of embedments in the Gazebo: tiles with hearts, seashells, pottery, colorful bits of glass in green and blue, and a golden bumble bee.

The north wall contains many fascinating decorations and embedments. Beginning at the west corner, you will find rows of corncobs, boots, and other shapes embellishing the colorful panels of the wall. The length of the north and south walls combined is almost 300 feet. The wall is decorated on both sides on the south and on the inside on the north.

The tower east of the Gazebo is the west tower the tallest at 99 and 1/2 feet high and the last tall tower built by the artist. Rodia built this tall tower and the others without use of a ladder or scaffold! A small man, about 5 feet tall, he waited until the cement hardened on the lower levels and then climbed up using the horizontal rings as his ladder rungs. Over his shoulder was a bag of dampened cement and a bag of decorations, and in one hand was a steel reinforcement. The foundation for this tallest tower is only 14 inches deep. Rodia dug a circular trench in the ground and put 16 pieces of steel - eight 2" X 2" X 1/4" angels and eight 2 1/2" X 2 1/2" X 5/16" T-sections - vertically in the trench at equal distances apart to form the reinforcements for the tower's 16 legs. Then he poured the concrete into the trench, forming a shell which included the 16 pieces of steel for the legs. He filled-in the open shell with broken concrete, covered the top of the shell to form the tower base and decorated the outside with his typical embedments. In some areas he added color to the cement or varied the surface finishes.

This tallest tower was subjected to a stress test simulating high wind loads on October 10, 1959 by and author of this article, to prove its strength and thus avoid demolition ordered by the Building and Safety Department of Los Angeles. The test was successful.

The center tower is 97 feet 10 inches tall. The tower consists of two separate sets of legs, forming a tower-within-a-tower design, unlike the west tower.

Between the center and east towers are a series of hearts on a set of connecting members, decorated with bottle glass and tiles.

The eastern tower is 55 feet tall and was the first tower Rodia made. On the north side, he built a ladder-like section extending to the top. This addition allowed easy access to the upper portions. Since the other two tall towers do not have built-in ladders, it may be assumed that Rodia found he could go up and down the sculptures with no trouble, even without a "ladder", by using the horizontal rings.

To the east of the east tower is the "Ship of Marco Polo" sculpture. The ship and its masts and superstructure are like all the Rodia works, different from the others. To the north of the ship, the wall contains sections of translucent glass inserts in orange and yellow which create a vivid display each day at sunset.

Rodia has left us with a wonderfully enjoyable work in the Watts Towers. Hidden among the many decorations are treasures you can find only by close observation. One such treasure, a delicate female form, was placed amidst a rock-filled wall panel in the south wall near the east tower.

Next time you visit the Towers, look for it.

VI

The Children and the Watts Towers Arts Center

by Rochelle Nicholas

Travelling south and central through Los Angeles, rising above the walkways, is an agitation of design. Security bar gates stripe weather beaten storefronts and the plywood patch plaid of deserted commercial space creates a ramshackle of color next to the festival of sidewalk thriftstore sales. Urban renewal is eminent in an environment programmed for decay. Still life clutter is the result of neglect. It is the livid appearance of broken promises of prosperity.

Neighborhoods parallel commercial thoroughfares. First necessity: security. Bars on windows, a church on every other corner. Located off Graham and 107th street is the Watts Towers Arts Center. The houses on both sides of the road are one story. Some are 1950's suburban tract stucco; others are old, very small, wooden two room cottages. Television aerials abound on roofs; partially working automobiles sit in driveways or are parked along the street. Most of the houses have small raised cement porches with an occasional creeper for shade. A small patch of grass, often bare earth, occupies the front of each fenced home. Faded wood picket, grey cement block, chain link wire, and near the end of the street, a frayed galvanized iron listing fence separates chickens and gardens from the yard of the adjacent home. A quiet family that has lived in the neighborhood for 14 years has just completed remodeling. The owners of the chicken farm have lived here 45 years. A record player plays.........child improvisations dart from between the houses......songs escape out into the night. It is a Charles Mingus lick, a Bearden painting, the train intruder as frame to a living portrait.

The White's chicken farm faces the Watts Towers. In 1956, on that side of the road, the small vacant house adjacent to the Towers became known as the Simon Rodia Art Center. Here, Rodia's work, his statement never stopped. As an emotionally charged symbol, it became a continuous portrait of the immigrant: lessons, stories and

Watts Towers' John Outterbridge with school kids from Center St. Elementary of El Segundo visiting the tower.

Sam Rodia's Watts Towers sends its sparkling spires almost 100 feet into the Los Angeles sky. Working alone over a thirty year span, with simple tools and no help. Rodia designed and erected in his side yard a remarkable act of visionary architecture he called 'Pueblo Nuestro' - Our Town.

Rodia built his Towers out of a selection of urban debris, including broken glazed tile, green Seven-Up and blue Milk of Magnesia bottle shards and other odds and ends he collected and carefully sorted in size and color. With these simple materials Rodia created dazzling patterns, enhanced by impressions of his tools pressed into wet cement.

The front gate to 'Pubelo Nuestro' - 1765 East 107th Street in Watts - is marked with Sam Rodia's initials in mosaic tile. An arch of green bottle bottoms frames the entry that led to the front door of Rodia's original wood-framed cottage, burned down in a 1955 fire after he left Los Angeles.

(ABOVE) A close-up of the canopy over the front gate displays an electric collection of mirror shards, tile pieces and bottle bottoms combined in a lacy cement design that seems casual yet is carefully designed to achieve a certain elegance.

(RIGHT) Radiating mosaic tiles framed by green Seven-Up bottle bottoms, chunks of melted glass and a conch shell decorate a panel of the triangular wall Rodia built to enclose his wedge-shaped lot. The sad attrition by both vandals and weather during the years of the Towers' neglect after Rodia left is seen in the smashed glass.

Sam Rodia's mail slot, made small to receive a lonely man's few letters. Amid the tiles and the glass are the impressions of flower-like faucet tops he pressed into wet cement.

(ABOVE) The underside of the entry canopy frames the vacant front door of Rodia's burned-out cottage. The canopy's sides and ceiling are decorated with whole plates, china unicorns, horses and dolls, and other witty bric-a-brac retrieved in Rodia's foraging along the nearby rail tracks.

(ABOVE) A detail of the Towers' cement floor showing the favorite heart shapes Rodia repeated in various materials throughout the complex. The delicacy of the floor designs point out the Towers' vulnerability to the scuffling shoes of the many visitors attracted to its wonders.

Looking into the Towers from the entry. The intricate "gazebo" with its lacy cement ribs and 40-foot-tall spire is seen to the left. The tallest tower, 97-foot 10-inches high, is in the background, behind the elaborate miniature foreground tower. This view reveals the subtle and complex interplay of thrusting and arching forms achieved in a compact space.

(ABOVE) The curve of the miniature tower and the edge of Rodia's ruined house frame the 'gazebo.' The way the constructions are laid out to half-hide the middle distance leads the eye to explore the shadows behind the curves, drawing the visitor deep into the heart of 'Nuestro Pubelo.'

(RIGHT) Steps at the base of the tallest West Tower helped Rodia climb up his construction. The form of these bases was probably remembered by Rodia from his childhood in a Southern Italian hilltop town, before he and his brother emigrated to America.

Looking down from above - a view Rodia often saw but visitors seldom enjoy -
reveals the pattern of slim ribs interconnecting all the Towers' various constructions.
These ribs add to the rich shadow play on the floor and walls.

Tower bases frame a view of the small fountain or front that some records say Rodia used in baptisimal rituals during a religious phase of his life. A social anarchist and a soul deeply influenced by the divine. Rodia struggled to resolve the paradoxes of the human condition and release his tensions in building the Towers.

Panels on the font's base are finished in crushed green glass. The north wall's undulating top protects the Towers from the now-disused rail spur that ran alongside. Over-arching ribs give the enclave a church-like ambiance suited to its quasi-religious function.

(ABOVE) Impressions of straw platters and jute-fibre doormats pressed into the cement add texture to the enclosing wall, enriching the pattern of embedded seashells, broken pottery and bits of tile. Intrigued by interesting tactile surfaces, Rodia sought ways to add them to the overall design.

(RIGHT) The base of the Middle Tower seems like a lava eruption. Round stones buried in cement modeled and pitted to resemble volcanic rocks anchor reinforced cement structural ribs circling a central column.

(LEFT) The outdoor oven where Rodia baked his bread could come straight out of the farm house of a Neapolitan peasant. The chimney is transformed into yet another delicate spire. The shelves for storing the cooling loaves have sides jewelled with fragments of stone and glass.

(BELOW) The rounded top of a wall panel shows how Rodia could bring life to every corner of his design. With a few shattered shards and bits of colored glass he contrived an elaboration that interests the eye without exhausting the viewer's attention.

The base of the Center Tower is built up of tiers of seashells, tile bottle bottoms, small rocks and embedded straw circles that seem to emerge like an array of natural forms from the patterned cement floor. This detail reveals the total integration of the Towers' structural system and decorative design.

(LEFT) The intricate incised patterning of this wall panel - created with impressions of faucet tops and decorative wrought-iron - conjure up an Islamic influence that may derive from the Saracen impact upon the region of Southern Italy where Rodia was born.

(BELOW) Rodia was employed for a time at the famous Malibu Potteries, where he may have collected this dazzling assemblage of vividly colored and patterned tile. The Towers are a repository of much of the early 20th century California tile work that graced so many Craftsman bungalows and Spanish Colonial Revival villas.

Stalagmites of crushed green glass, mini-spires of seashells and tiled ribs lighten the strong base forms of the miniature tower and 'cactus garden' featured near the entrance.

A ladder of hearts decorates the flying ribs that connect the Center and East Towers. The ribs are both a structural bracing and a charming silhouette against the blue heavens; they reveal Rodia's intuitive grasp of the fusion of form and feeling.

Rodia started building the Towers from the prow of the east wall with this 'Ship or Marco Polo.' On a small and simple scale the designer experimented with the construction and decoration of the spires and miniatures he would later enlarge and elaborate elsewhere in the Towers.

(ABOVE) This tower core detail resembles the tiered fountains that grace the piazzas of many Mediterranean towns. Though waterless, the decorated tiers lighten the muscularity of the structural shaft and make it seem almost playful.

(LEFT) One may imagine a popular small-town orator making an impassioned speech from the colorful podium created by these tower steps in the mini-piazza of 'Nuestro Pueblo.' The Malibu tilework in the treads and risers give the solid steps a lightness of spirit.

'SR, NUESTRA PUEBLO, 1921' is the message spelled out in the mosaic on a cement rung of the West Tower. Rodia was vague with dates, and it may be that he started constructing the Towers five or six years later than 1921.

The intricacy and lightness of the Towers is remarkable. As he worked from east to west, Rodia gradually and pragmatically made his structures more slender, growing more and more in tune with the inherent strength of the construction system he had devised. The West Tower, shown here, is both the tallest and the lightest of the three main spires.

(ABOVE) The Malibu Potteries functioned for a very short period, from 1926-32, but its impact was profound. Other California tile makers imitated its popular designs, that featured the strong colors and vivid geometric patterns that so attracted Rodia.

(BELOW) The East Tower's construction is the least adventurous. The central shaft is thick and the outside struts are skinny and merely decorative. In this early construction the charm is there but the structural grace is yet to evolve.

The Rococo fusion of tracery and decoration is dramatized in this detail of the West Tower. Every aspect of the design combined to create a sense of joyous uplift as the open-webbed shaft surges skywards in a burst of color and delicate structure.

(RIGHT) This wall panel detail demonstrates Rodia's delight and skill in mixing disparate materials, including patterned tiles, mother-of-pearl, volcanic rock and common seashells.

(BELOW) The south wall is richly decorated with tiles, rocks, incised patterns and raised designs. In the strong Angeleno sunlight, whose sparkle reminded Rodia of his Mediterranean homeland, the vivid colors and bas-relief shapes dazzle the eye.

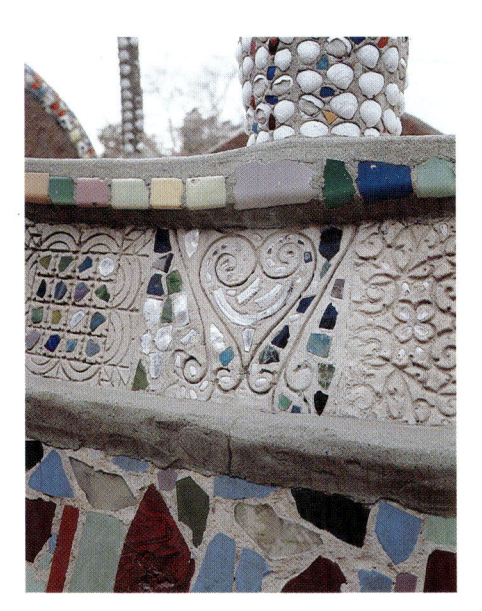

(ABOVE) Molten glass, green glazed bottle pieces, blue Milk of Magnesia glass and mosaic tile are shaped into circular designs that contrast with the adobe-like texture of the rough cement wall.

(LEFT) The conjunction of different decorative materials and incised patterns is skilfully handled in a small space. The richness gives energy to the surface without sliding into kitsch, as it may have done in less sensitive hands.

Rodia was a small man, barely five feet tall, and he constructed his Towers by reaching from one rung to the next. This reach sets the rhythm of the horizontal rungs that gives the spires their profoundly human scale as they soar skyward.

ABOVE) Looking over the top of the South wall you see the spires and curves beyond. Note how the relief designs on the wall mimic the arches of the towers and create a sense of walking down an Italian city street.

(LEFT) Mussel shells seem like the scales on the leg of some primeval monster beside Sam Rodia's signature.

The 'volcanic' effect in detail at the base of the Center Tower - an upthrust of energy expressed in cement and rock.

(ABOVE) Sam Rodia's proud impulse to write his name all over the Towers is kin to the urge that impels those gang graffiti writers who cover the walls of Watts with their markers - markers which proclaim. "This is my territory! I was here!"

A large chunk of found tilework with a peacock pattern is melted into the design, set off by floor tile and mosaics.

The three main towers march down towards the Watts horizon like sentries on guard against the urban despair that surrounds "Nustero Pueblo" on all sides.

At sunrise Sam Rodia's magic spires become a truly visionary architecture - a golden tracery that hymns the hopes of the human spirit.

hearsay; opinions, the force of circumstance, evidence of change. All was reflected in the face of the Towers and recognized by an array of citizens.

The City of Los Angeles acquired the Watts Towers properties to continually preserve Rodia's construct and focus attention on art and the cultural histories of South-Central Los Angeles. The municipally funded Watts Towers Arts Center serves the community, it is a vital complement to the Rodia Towers.

Its physically facility consists of a 2,000-square-foot center gallery, a north and south gallery approximately 500 square feet, and two offices used also for storage and reception.

The Education Program looks at the explicative relationships between art and society. Programming includes: scheduled tours, changing gallery exhibits, lectures; a visiting schools as well as neighboring schools program and two annual Heritage Festivals which attract a growing and diverse audience in the thousands.

Director John Outterbridge is a conceptual artist. The portrait of the community encourages, and sometimes compromises, his ability to create. Devoted to humanity, John is closely associated with a circle of thinkers and social reformers. Education programming becomes an artistic collaboration as each contributes skill and effort in view of society and from a personal perspective of a contemporary situation.

Students, kindergarten through university level, are involved in the dialectical relationship with works of art. Through inquiry, experimental games and related historical input, students attempt to interpret and give as much meaning to the work of art as any artist would. The teachers task becomes one of expanding the student's perspective of a given work of art, beyond its historical, political and social bounds.

A tour of the Towers reveals a portrait of an artist, his position within the cultural and aesthetic currents, and an interplay with the history of his surroundings.

Walk again through the community. At street level, pass through the lingering shadow of the past.

Today Watts is under more pressure than in 1955: massive unemployment, narcotics saturation, police oppression, inadequate schools and housing. The socio-cultural facilities that arose from the 1965 revolt were: the Studio Watts Workshop, the Mafundi Institute, Westminister Neighborhood Association, Frederick Douglas Writer's Hose, the Meeting at the Watts Towers, the Community Arts and Crafts Council and the Coffee House. The present shopping mall on 103rd street replaced the old merchant district and Martin Luther King Hospital was Palm Lane Housing. New township concepts exist for seniors and extend to others. The remaining cultural arts facility is the Art Center, functioning out of a rudimentary building.

Consequently, we, the Watts Towers Arts Center, recognize and accept the nature of the challenge: the survival and preservation of socio-cultural institutions propagated in the arts and born out of local human circumstance; the reassembling of historical fragments to be woven in the new faces of art. And the children are educated by incident of proximity. They are ever present.

Rochelle Nicholas   1987

John Outterbridge conducts an Arts Center painting class.

SABATO ALONE

by John Outterbridge

YELLOW brown weed fields
green of Mudtown memories
and lemon grass jungles grown
WILD old red car rails rusted
deep the station house graffiti
RAPS grey sparrows dusty rise
through cobalt blue sky above
SUNBLUSHED dandelions push pass
asphalt blackened patches cracked
glass kaleidoscopes race like iridescent silver fish
LEAKY roofs weep morning rain
drenched hand fixed castles colored
BRIGHT the charm of children's jump rope
play on wind blown runs of dogs gone stray
and crow the cocks at break of day

SABATO ALONE
the moonshine sipping spirit catcher
electric fire song maker highrising mode breaker
SABATO ALONE
the totesack tipsy patchworking polychromed angel flights
SABATO ALONE
the mud bucket purple glazed harlequin mountain climber
born again for the sake of a child's third eye dreaming
SABATO ALONE
the elevated Lord Master of 107 million cosmic visions rescued
from the quaking seize of the BUREAU'S grasp
SABATO ALONE
the uphoisted GURU of the RAINBOW SKY TRIBE'S
majestic spiraling mantras
made for themselves oneness renamed
SABATO ALONE

LOS ANGELES SCHOOLS' WATTS TOWERS COMPETITION, MAY 1985.

Los Angeles. school girl draws a version of a personal Watts Towers.

In May 1985 The Herald Examiner sponsored a contest among Junior High Schools in the Los Angeles Unified School District to "construct models reflecting the spirit of Sam Rodia's Towers in Watts." Prizes of $1,000, $500 and $250 were offered to the winners, plus a chance to display all the finalist entries at the Museum of Contemporary Art's Temporary Contemporary Gallery in Little Tokyo. Fourteen final designs were chosen, made by students who worked either as individuals or in groups. All entries interpreted the Towers in ways that rivaled the creative instincts of Rodia himself. Each Reflected a particular neighborhood, ethnic background and perspective on Los Angeles. Entrants were asked to interpret the spirit of theTowers, not just copy its distinctive style . The results were extraordinary. First prize went to Belvedere Junior High for a pair of linked Towers pasted over with newspaper and magazine photos rising out of a L.A. street map surrounded by a brick wall displaying graffitti. "We discussed issues and concerns," said Belvedere Art teacher Johann Hassan. "We made a social statement ." Mid-City Alternative Junior High placed second with its imaginative composition featuring a floating half-orange. Hollenbeck Junior School placed third with a tower of strawberry punnets reaching skywards. Other Highly original entries came from King Junior High (two submissions), Carver Junior High, Virgil Junior High, Berendo Junior High, Muir Junior High, Wilmington Junior High, Gompers Junior High, Hale Junior High, Millikan Junior High, and Harte Preparatory Intermidiate. Entries were judged by MOCA Director Richard Koshalek, Michael Pittas, Dean of Otis/Parsons School of Design and Herald Art Critic Christopher Knight.

VII

The Towers As Art

Christopher Knight, Art Critic

The French filmmaker Louis Malle once said something that, in a flash, made me think of the extraordinary pull on the imagination exerted by Sam Rodia's famous Towers in Watts. Malle, who had been a permanent resident (although not a citizen) of this country for more than five years, and who thus had experienced the immigrant's dislocated sense of being neither a true outsider nor a true insider in the host culture, was talking about the difficult problem of feeling that he belonged.

"I think this country is a country of drifters," Malle told a reporter for the New York Times. "It's one of the few general statements I could permit myself about America. It seems that people here, they don't really have roots, and at least part of the population (has) been all over the place. They were not born here. It's such a mobile population."

Like hundreds of thousands of others, Sam Rodia was an immigrant, too. And for almost all of the first 30 years the Italian-born laborer spent in America, he was a relentless drifter. First he followed his brothers to the coal fields of Pennsylvania, then he journeyed on his own to the Northwest coast and the city of Seattle, and next he moved to the small town of Fruitvale in the Bay Area. Nobody seems to know quite where this self-appointed gypsy wandered next - Texas? Mexico? Wisconsin? - but he resurfaced in Southern California in 1918 and stayed for nearly four decades. Within five or six years of his arrival, he had begun, quite suddenly, to work on the dazzling monument that now occupies a small triangular plot of land in the neighborhood of Watts.

It would be difficult to name a place anywhere in America that is a more pertinent example of Louis Malle's observations than Los Angeles, the city in which Rodia finally chose to settle. In both geography and population, it is the quintessential city of rootlessness and mobility for the 20th-century. And the neighborhood of Watts - a flat horizonless expanse dotted with small buildings and crisscrossed by the railroad tracks on which generations of immigrants came into the region - was a place where Latinos and Anglos and blacks and Japanese lived side by side in the 1920s. It was here that Rodia the drifter set about constructing a microcosmic village - Nuestro Pueblo, or Our Town, he pointedly called it - a place where he literally could live, could re-create his roots, and could enshrine the memories and experiences of his life.

Within the high, medieval walls that enclosed his "town," Sam Rodia could belong.

Like the town hall or cathedral spires of a medieval Italian city, the delicate tracery of Rodia's three towers at once identifies the place as a safe haven from the indifferent chaos of the world that surrounds them, and simultaneously provides a high promontory that separates the place from that decidedly different realm outside. Coupled with the walled, triangular form of Nuestro Pueblo, the towers also result in a configuration reminiscent of a three-masted sailing ship that has been frozen in place, never to sail again - except in the imagination. (Not surprisingly, Rodia's ancestral countryman and fellow wanderer, Christopher Columbus, stood high among the immigrant's heroes.) Encrusted with bits of green 7-UP and blue Milk of Magnesia bottles, with shards of broken pottery and seashells, and printed with impressions of the simple tools Rodia used to build the structure, they're the grand residue of a private, celebratory ritual devoted to the regeneration of the natural and vernacular artifacts of life.

The layers of reference embedded in the Watts Towers are seemingly endless and inclusive, yet they all speak of a conflicting experience that strikes to the very core of 20th-century life. The most basic human experience that is given form by this magnificent place is the conflict and tension between the deep desire to belong and the profound need to separate. Rodia built a home, a place of belonging whose permanence and multiple historical allusions were all directly connected to his memories, to his life, to himself. And he did it in a way that was like no other, one that distinguished both the endeavour and the maker from everything and everyone else.

For Rodia, the rootlessness and mobility that informed his life as an immigrant, and that were (and remain) so fundamental to the ethnics of Los Angeles, were no doubt thrown into high relief when compared with his own origins. He was born in Rivotoli, a small village in Southern Italy where the sense of rootedness, of ancientness is embedded in every stone. Rivotoli is in the province of Campania, the very region so beloved by such 19th-century American painters as Thomas Cole, John F. Kensett and George Inness. These painters, who were themselves living on a vast new continent where the most visible signs of history were the ancient trees, approached their voyages to the Campania as quite literal pilgrimages to the lost classical cradle of Western civilization. For in the New World they, too stood apart and separate from their past, and they wanted to belong. The raw, untouched landscape of America was shining evidence of their natural genesis, but the rolling hills, medieval villages and ancient ruins of the Campania spoke tellingly of cultural origins. To this natural/cultural wellspring they added concentrated study of the European traditions of art, especially landscape painting, of Constable and Claude and the 17th-century Dutch. In their finest paintings, the vernacular imagery of their new land reverberates against a vivid and articulate language of self-conscious cultural memory.

Into the Mediterranean climate of the Los Angeles basin Sam Rodia brought the traces of that legacy. Although it's doubtful that he could either read or write, his was nevertheless a vivid and articulate language of unselfconscious personal memory. Inflected and enriched by the vernacular of his new home, Rodia's procedure differed radically from that employed by 19th-century painters who crossed the Atlantic in search of cultural origins. And that difference is what makes his monumental achievement a masterful work of folk art.

I've often wondered whether this simple fact has been one primary contributor to the awful neglect suffered by the Watts Towers. For it is often foolishly believed that folk art is not quite up to snuff - not quite "real" art. Yet the brilliance of Rodia's Towers is found in the degree to which the structure bores so deeply into the individual and collective feeling of American life, the degree to which it is art. That the language of forms Rodia used is a folk or vernacular idiom, rather than the self-conscious traditions of modern art, in no way diminishes the magnitude of his utterance or the power of his speech. It merely means the chosen forms, language, traditions, rituals and ways of revealing the tensions embodied in finding one's place in the world are different. The Watts Towers belongs to art of a distinctive kind.

This distinction between folk art and other kinds of art is, I believe, much more than a semantic argument. For, quite frankly that vivifying quality of coexisting difference is - or should be - one of the fundamental beauties of Nuestro Pueblo.

VIII

The Musicians of Watts Towers

Mikal Gilmore,
Music Critic.

In his rollicking, scathing and memorable imaginative autobiography, jazz composer and bassist Charles Mingus wrote about afternoons spent in his youth, watching Sam Rodia as he went about his patient, complex work of building, transforming, tearing down then rebuilding the bizarre spirals known today as the Watts Towers.

Mingus - who was born in Arizona and had moved to Watts with his family as a child remembered the construction largely as a funny, mutable and devout process: One day, he said, you would pass by and a new tower would be jutting into the sky, like a sharp barb against Watts' low profile. The next day, you would walk past and the tower would be gone, plucked out of the work, just as a phrase that didn't set quite right in the overall harmony of a piece might be removed by a musician. Mingus thought all this was a little crazy, but also beautiful and inspiring, and when neighborhood kids would taunt Rodia, it moved him to sadness.

Years later, after he had been to New York and met Charlie Parker, Bud Powell, Thelonius Monk and Max Roach, Mingus returned to L.A. to play clubs in the Watts and South-Central areas, and sometimes at night, carrying his upright bass, he would go past the nearly finished Towers. It struck him on one of these occasions, he later said, that Rodia's Towers was much like the impulsive but meticulously structured music he had just been playing - that is, is was a resourceful and vital work, an invention for freedom and transcendence.

Mingus, of course, was one of the more significant and better-known musicians to emerge from Watts - though, in truth, because he moved to New York early in his career and recorded there much of his life, he is almost never remembered as a Los Angeles musician. Indeed, surprisingly little critical or popular attention has ever been paid to Watts' (or L.A.'s) standing as an essential and productive

The annual Watts Towers Jazz Festival draws a crowd.

scene in the evolution of jazz and R&B. Yet, during the crucial passages between the demise of the big hands and the rise of bop and cool, and between the end of World War II and the mid-'50s explosion of rock 'n' roll (and, consequently, the fusion and eruption of youth, black and pop culture), Watts played a key and transformative role - the meeting place for a necessary colloquy among jazz, blues and R&B that could never have occurred in New York, Chicago, Kansas City, Detroit or Memphis. In fact, like New Orleans, Watts (which had more than tripled its black population during the '40s) was a birthplace for R&B: It was here that blues and jazz met, mingled and committed a lustful union that eventually spawned a wildly popular and fervid new form though few pop historians have documented that event. Like Rodia's Towers, the community's legacy has too long been neglected.

If one had to pick a representative figure of this period, it may as well be Johnny Otis - the Berkeley-born drummer and pianist who led a rousing blues-and-swing big hand throughout California and the Southwest during the mid-'40s, before settling down in Watts with a stripped-down nine-piece group that became a model for R&B ensembles. In part, one cites Otis because his musical development reflected the direction black popular music would take in this time and place (though he was hardly seminal: Texas-born T-Bone Walker - the first bluesman to define a style on electric guitar - had also played in big bands and then moved to a smaller-scale sound, and had been a force on the Watts scene since the '30s). More important, though, Otis was one of the few musicians or musicologists to seem to have understood what was happening in Watts and L.A. - what it was that set the scene apart from any other American urban center.

"The only explanation I can offer," he told critic Pete Welding, "is that the cats around Chicago came from the Delta of Mississippi Tennessee and around there. Our guys came from Oklahoma and Texas and there was a difference. Our California blues style was a Texas-Oklahoma combination, that Southwestern influence. And it was a very different tradition they drew on, the swing band thing...The guy who started it all, T-Bone Walker...now, he was a Texan.

"Charles Brown, who did this thing that penetrated so deeply into all our consciousness, is a Texan. Joe Liggins is, I believe, from Oklahoma, and Roy Milton, too. Eddie 'Cleanhead' Vinson is a Texan. A Texas-Oklahoma thing is what happened here."

Looking back over accounts of the '40s music scene that reached from Watts and South-Central L.A. to Hollywood and occasionally Santa Monica, it is intriguing to see just how actively Otis figured in it. Indeed, in addition to his regular appearances at the city's leading black nightclubs (including Club Alabam, Cherryland, Black Dot McGhee's) and operating his own hopping joint (the Barrelhouse), Otis' ties seem to lead everywhere: to definitive "honker" saxophonist Illinois Jacquet, whom many consider the single most forceful link between jazz and rock style, and with whom Otis sometimes recorded; to the Robins, the vocal group he employed in the early '50s, who shortly went on to become the Coasters; to Little Richard, who briefly fronted Otis' band in the mid-'50s; and, most famously, to Little Esther Phillips, the 13-year-old Dinah Washington-influenced blues-jazz-R&B singer whom he made his star attraction in the late '40s, and who went on to make periodically compelling soul-pop recordings through the late '70s.(Following Phillips' death last August at age 48, the Rev. Johnny Otis presided at her funeral. "She was a woman of wit, of grace and of powerful presence," he noted at the time. "Esther personified that melancholy power of the blues.")

Perhaps Otis' most transient but significant tie was to Jerry Leiber and Mike Stoller: two East Coast-born white songwriters who had dreams of reinventing the Tin Pan Alley tradition, but who also had strong political and aesthetic tastes for black music - most notably, the blues. Leiber and Stoller revised their ambitions after visiting several Watts and South-Central clubs, where they saw how Otis and many others were transforming the potential of American pop music at large. During the '50s, the two would take what they had learned from the Watts scene and begin to codify it into a songcraft. Indeed, they were R&B and rock 'n' roll's first great auteurs - melding Tin Pan alley and blues styles into a new, radical and enduring song form that was ambitious pop, but also genuine art. Over the years they would write songs for Ray Charles, Charles Brown, Ben E. King ("Stand by Me" and "Spanish Harlem"), Dion ("Ruby Baby"), Little Willie Littlefield ("Kansas City"), LeVern Baker ("Saved"), the Drifters ("Dance With Me" and "There Goes My Baby") and Big Mama Thornton ("Hound Dog" - which was the pair's first production effort, and which featured Otis on the drums).

But Leiber and Stoller's most important advancement of R&B came with L.A.'s Coasters, who, like the Robins, had worked in the late '40s as a vocal quartet with Otis and Leiber and Stoller and the Coasters gave the first massively popular voice to black social concerns with such songs as "Charles Brown," "Down in Mexico," "Run, Red, Run," "Along Came Jones," "Riot in Cell Block #9" and

Annual Watts Towers Jazz Festival in July.
At piano, band leader Johnny Otis.

"Framed" - many of which were received largely as comedic numbers, though they all had a purposeful political subtext. With Leiber and Stoller the Coasters became America's most popular pop, R&B and rock group of the '50s. Indeed, the only bigger event was Elvis Presley, who liked Leiber and Stoller's work so much he hired them to write the music for his best films: "Love Me Tender," "Loving You," "King Creole" and "Jailhouse Rock." By the end of the '50s, the legacy of Watts and South-Central's music had been transmogrified and had reached around the globe with indelible effect. While Leiber and Stoller were always honest and mindful about what they had drawn from that scene, Watts' importance still went largely unnoted.

But the blues and R&B were only half the story: Watts, South Central and Hollywood also hosted an active jazz life that for a time could rival anything heard on New York's 52nd Street, or in Kansas City or New Orleans. In fact, when Charlie "Bird" Parker and Dizzy Gillespie - the kingpins of hop - visited in 1946, they discovered that their radical innovations in rhythm and melody had caught on in the local community like a welcome   - emulated and advanced by such distinctive and powerful saxophonists as Lucky Thompson, Sonny Criss, Dexter Gordon and Wardell Gray. Parker, in fact, wold record some of his most inventive and legendary sessions for Dial during his stay, with sidemen that included Thompson and Miles Davis. Unfortunately, Bird would also steepen his drug problems while here, and eventually was confined briefly to the psychiatric ward at the L.A. County Jail, then remained to Camarillo State Hospital, where he spent seven months.

But according to some witnesses, during Bird's initial stay in early 1946, the Los Angeles black music scene hit an unbelievable peak - and jazz, blues and R&B musicians interacted with an exhilarating openness. One critic even reports that there was a season when a fan could club hop back and forth between Club Alabam, Lovejoy, Down Beat, Savoy, Memo and Last Word on Central Avenue or up the street to Jack's Basket, or even over to Billy Berg's in Hollywood, and on the right night or two, one might catch Bird, Gillespie or Mingus, as well as (hold your breath!) Milt Jackson, Ray Brown, Hampton Hawes, Sonny Criss, Dexter Gordon, Wardell Gray, Illinois and Russell Jacquet, T-Bone Walker, Art Farmer, Oscar Pettiford or Nat King Cole's trios, Helen Humes, Slim Gaillard, Jay McShann, Roy Milton, Eddie "Cleanhead" Vinson, Joe Turner, Joe Liggins, Wynonie Harris and, of course, Johnny Otis and his band. While it's unlikely that all these artists ever played in this city on the same night - or even during the same few weeks - it is nonetheless true that they all played in Watts and Los Angeles with some regularity during the late '40s, and that alone is remarkable news.

One could go on - for example, in the '50s both Ornette Coleman and Art Pepper developed the essential styles and theories of their art while playing many of those same clubs, and in their early records, one can hear them flailing against the gradual calcification of the scene - but the short (though hardly simple) truth is that even L.A. didn't know what a treasure it had in the music of Watts and South-Central. In time, many of the best talents left, and the area itself get hemmed in by freeways, indifference, neglect and racial fear.

Currently, however, the L.A. pop scene is witnessing a wonderful resurgence of interest in R&B and "roots"-style music - and not merely from the nostalgist's or revivalist's point of view. To be sure, some of this affection is directed toward the many fine surviving blues and R&B greats who recently have made L.A. a home or regular stopover. The increasing local awareness of L.A.'s native blues and R&B treasurers also owes much to the scrupulousness of such local young talents as the Blasters, X, Los Lobos, Steve Berlin, Top Jimmy, Carlos Guitarlos, Melvis and the Megatones and other, plus a great debt to the efforts of the Southern California Blues Society, which often presents shows at the Music Machine, the Central and Berwin's.

Clora Bryant

The annual Watts Day of the Drum sends out a powerful beat.

Here's a brief list of some of the best music of Watts. Not all of it was recorded in Los Angeles, but none of it would be possible without the spirit of that scene, as it was felt during its '40s and '50s peak:

The Coasters, "Young Blood" (Atlantic)
Ornette Coleman, "Something Else" (Contemporary)
Sonny Criss and others, "Black California" (Savoy)
Dexter Gordon and Wardell Gray, "The Hunt" (Savoy)
Amos Milburn, "Chicken Shack Boogie" (Aladdin Import)
Johnny Otis, "The Original Johnny Otis Show" (Savoy)
Charlie Parker, "The Very Best of Bird" (Warner Bros.)
Art Pepper, "Smack Up" (Contemporary)
Little Esther Phillips, "The Complete Savoy Recordings" (Savoy)
Joe Turner, "Have No Fear, Big Joe Turner Is Here" (Savoy)
T-Bone Walker, "Classics of Modern Blues" (Blue Note)

Los Angeles Schools' Watts Towers Competition, May 1985

Appendix A

Conservation Challenges
Bud Goldstone
1959-1991

Vandalism and the environment have caused great loss to the Watts Towers over the years since Rodia created the sculptures. Perhaps twenty percent of the decorations in the mortar covers are broken and another five percent are gone from their original installations. Visitors constantly ask: "Are they going to replace the 7-UP bottles, the sea shells, the pottery, and the tiles so the Towers will look new, again?". The answer is not easy.

Conservation and "restoration" of the Watts Towers have been subjects of considerable controversy since 1959 between members of the art community and interested laymen. The art community generally supports the scheme that "repairs" made to the sculptures of Rodia should be easily differentiated from the artist's work. Furthermore they believe that objects imbedded in the mortar of the work which are broken or missing should not be replaced with other embedments unless clear documentation exists of the original embedment. "When conjecture begins, restoration ends" said one of these experts. Laymen and some artists and architects want the Towers restored so they will look new again.

During early conservation repairs by the State of California under a 1979 "Conservation Plan" no embedments were replaced and all repair mortar was colored gray and recessed from the original sculptural outline of the Rodia work for easy identification. But in 1984 and 1985, the last two years of the State's $1,200,00 repair project on the three tall towers, damaged or missing embedments were replaced or added to the sculpture and replacement mortar was applied to match the original shape, texture, and color of sculptured members.

These changes were recommended by the State's consultant, The Ehrenkrantz Group, which had been subjected to a great deal of vocal pressure by the Board of the Committee for Simon Rodia's Towers in Watts, a citizen group which has acted as watchdog to the Towers since 1959. The authority for the change was published in 1982 in a newly commissioned preliminary version of a "Conservation Plan" and later in the 1984 final issue of the document. During 1983 and 1984, the State restoration crew, following the new official position, purchased and applied glass, tiles, sea shells, and colored mortar to the sculptures.

Historically, the damage to the structures has consisted of cracked or deteriorated mortar which forms the cover over the metal reinforcements, and rusted or deteriorated wire mesh and reinforcements which have become exposed by the failure of the mortar cover. Additionally, decorative inserts have deteriorated or become dislodged or broken by natural effects or vandalism. It is known that Rodia performed many crack-filling operations on the mortar in various locations in the 3 tall towers, often covering cracked members with new mortar, wire mesh, and decorative inserts. A City of Los Angeles Inspector indicated Rodia did repair work as early as 1946.

In 1959, a large quantity of mortar and decoration - sea shells, tile, glass, and small members, "debris" - had accumulated on the patio floor in the 4 years since Rodia left the site. Between 1959 and 1978, even after repairs had been made, small decorative pieces and bits of mortar covering regularly became dislodged, most often after rains and high winds followed by sunny days.

In late 1977/early 1978 after local record rains and winds, a large quantity of "debris" began falling from the structures - primarily from the 3 tall towers. In early March 1978, several large members fell from the structures when the reinforcements failed due to deterioration and a resultant lack of strength.

A major crack-filling and waterproofing job was funded by the Committee for Simon Rodia's Towers in Watts (CSRTW) and performed in late 1959/early 1960 under order from the Los Angeles Building and Safety Department. Similar crack-filling/ waterproofing jobs were performed during the period 1963 to 1972 by Williams Waterproofing Company. No effort was made to replace metal reinforcements until the State of California repairs, starting in May 1979.

On May 8, 1979, the State of California, Department of Parks and Recreation issued the Conservation and Maintenance Plan (5 pages) and Specifications - Emergency Repair and Conservation - Simon Rodia's Towers Watts, California (6 pages) which were to control the work done by restoration specialists from the California Office of the State Architect. In early October 1979, Amendment #1 to the original requirements documents was issued, defining reinforcement cleaning and treatment. These documents were developed by the State with inputs from representatives of the J. Paul Getty Museum; the National Trust for Historic Preservation; CSRTW; and the City of Los Angeles.

This work extended over 74 months, cost $1,200,000, and resulted in extensive mortar, wire mesh, and metal reinforcement repairs and replacements in each of the three tall towers, and a complete waterproofing application to each tower. Some work was also done to the arched legs of the Gazebo and the north wall but none to the other sculptures. Six different on-site State supervisors and almost 20 different crew members had been involved in the job in crews from a low of 1 to a peak in 1985 of 10 men.

In mid-1983, after completion of work by the State on the east (55 feet high) tower, much of the center (97 feet 10 inch) tower, and portions of the west (99 feet 6 inch) tower; modifications to the repair techniques were recommended through findings by The Ehrenkrantz Group (under contract to the State Department of Parks and Recreation). These changes were gradually introduced to the State restoration crew which modified some techniques. The specific modifications made, when they were made, and for which type of repairs, are not well documented. However, recommendations for change are specified in the 2 Ehrenkrantz Group volumes: Preservation Plan (238 pages) and in the Maintenance and Restoration Guide (72 pages), which were finally released in mid 1984, 5 years after repairs had begun and 14 months before work was ended by the State.

In 1978 Watts Towers was closed to the public to allow for major repairs to the kind of structural cracks shown here.

STATUS OF REPAIRS AND FUTURE PLANS DECEMBER 1986

3 Tall Towers

The damaged members of the 3 tall towers have been extensively repaired by replacements of rusted steel reinforcements with stainless steel structure and wire mesh in hundreds of feet of the columns, bands, braces, and spokes. Repair, replacement or resurfacing of the mortar covers have been accomplished in the same areas and in other areas of the structures. Repair documentation consists of daily and monthly progress reports during the 74 month period, and a repair log with 2, 900 photographs taken of hundreds of individual repairs. Other records of materials procurement, scaffolding, fencing, etc. are held by the State.

City Conservation Program 1986-1991

The City of Los Angeles program for conservation of the Rodia Towers was begun in December 1985, in a five phase series of projects with a 5-year trust fund established to finance the work.

Phase one has involved establishing 24-hour site security and regular site maintenance, removal of graffiti, computerized filing of the State's 2,900 repair photographs, and development of preliminary requirement specifications for the remaining phases of the conservation. A protective fence and security lighting design for the site is planned.

Phase two, beginning in January 1987, will acquire a set of archival baseline photographs of the Towers; phase three, also starting in 1987, will be a thorough visual inspection; phase four will consist of emergency conservation efforts; and phase five will be a comprehensive conservation of the entire monument. The total cost is not known, but the 5-year $800,000 fund set aside by the City will probably not cover all necessary work.

The exact conservation-restoration approach which will be taken by the City is not known at this time, but they plan to follow the advice of the art community in the first four phases including the emergency conservation. Then the City may entertain "restoration" proposals for portions of the Towers. Restoration will require funding, and the availability of skilled conservation personnel to accomplish the challenging task.

STATUS OF THE WATTS TOWERS AND THE SITE
Reporting by N.J. Goldstone, 10/1/85

Background:

Historically, the damage to the structures has consisted of cracked/deteriorated mortar which forms the cover over the metal reinforcements, and rusted/deteriorated wire mesh and reinforcements which have become exposed by the failure of the mortar cover. Additionally, decorative inserts have deteriorated and/or become dislodged by natural effects or vandalism. It is known that Rodia performed many crack/filling operations on the mortar in various locations in the 3 tall towers, often covering cracked members with new mortar, wire mesh, and decorative inserts. City of Los Angeles inspectors indicated Rodia did repair work as early as 1946.

In 1959, a large quantity of mortar and decorations - sea shells, tile, glass, and small members, "debris" - had accumulated on the patio floor in the 4 years since Rodia left the site. Between 1959 and 1978, even after repairs had been made, small decorative pieces and bits of mortar covering regularly became dislodged, most often after rains and high winds followed by sunny days.

In late 1977/early 1978 after local record rains and winds, a large quantity of "debris" began falling from the structures - primarily from the 3 tall towers. In early March 1978, several large members fell from the structures when the reinforcements failed due to deterioration and a resultant lack of strength.

REPAIR HISTORY
October 1959-1978

A major crack-filling and waterproofing job was funded by the Committee for Simon Rodia's Towers in Watts (CSRTW) and performed in late 1959/early 1960 under order from the Los Angeles Building and Safety Department. Similar crack-filling/waterproofing jobs were performed during the period 1963 to 1972 by Williams Waterproofing Company. No effort was made to replace metal reinforcements until the State of California repairs, starting in May 1979.

The 'financially feasible' conservation theory arrived at by the CSRTW and L.A. Building and Safety in 1959 was that if the structural continuity and integrity of the mortar covers were maintained, and if water intrusion through the covers was minimized, the life of the structures would be maximized.

A stress recording instrument *(arrow)* is adjusted by engineer today as "torture testing" of the controversial Watts Towers begins. Nearby a monster crane is exerting 10,000 pounds of pulling pressure on the tower. If it stands up under this pull, all towers will be allowed to remain as monuments to American art.

REPAIR HISTORY
May 1979-July 1985

On May 8, 1979, the State of California, Department of Parks and Recreation issued the Conservation and Maintenance Plan and Specifications - Emergency Repair and Conservation - for Rodia's Towers in Watts, which were to control the work done by restoration specialists from the California Office of the State Architect. In early October 1979, Amendment #1 to the original requirements documents was issued, defining reinforcement cleaning and treatment. These documents were developed by the State with inputs from representatives of the J. Paul Getty Museum/the National Trust for Historic Preservation, and the City of Los Angeles.

This work extended over 74 months, cost $1,200,000, and resulted in extensive mortar, wire mesh, and metal reinforcement repairs and replacements in each of the three tall towers, and a complete waterproofing application to each tower. Some work was also done to the arched legs of the Gazebo and the north wall but none to the other sculptures. Six different on-

The controversial Watts Towers stood fast under a pressure pull of 10,000 lb. and the city Departmernt of Building and Public Safety conceded that they are not dangerous and will be permitted to stay. The city had moved to tear down the structures and had ignited a civic controversy.

site State supervisors and almost 20 different crew members had been involved in the job in crews from a low of 1 to a peak in 1985 of 10 men.

In mid-1983, after completion of work by the State on the east (55 feet high) tower, such of the center (97 feet 10 inch) tower, and portions of the west (99 feet 6 inch) tower, modifications to the repair techniques were recommended through findings by The Ehrenkrantz Group (under contract to the State Department of Parks and Recreation). These changes were gradually introduced to the State restoration crew which modified some techniques. The specific modifications made, when they were made, and for which type of repairs, are not well documented, if at all. However, recommendations for change are specified in the 2 Ehrenkrantz Group volumes: Preservation Plan (238 pages) and in the Maintenance and Restoration Guide (72 pages), which were finally released in mid-1984, 5 years after repairs had begun and 14 months before work was ended by the State.

STATUS OF REPAIRS and FUTURE PLANS

3 Tall Towers

The damaged members of the 3 tall towers have been extensively repaired by replacements of rusted steel reinforcements with stainless steel structure and wire mesh in hundreds of feet of the columns, bands, braces, and spokes. Repair, replacement or resurfacing of the mortar covers have been accomplished in the same areas and in other areas of the structures. Repair documentation which is available in Los Angeles, consists of daily and monthly progress reports during the 74 month period, and a repair log with several thousand photographs taken of hundreds of individual repairs. Other records of materials procurement, scaffolding, fencing, etc. may be held by the State.

OTHER SITE SCULPTURES

The other Rodia sculptures on the site include: the Gazebo; Ship of Marco Polo; remains of Rodia's house; other structures; patio; overhead connectors; and the wall.

The structural condition of these sculptures ranges from good to poor. The repairs specified in the State of California May 1979 and the Ehrenkrantz documents for the other sculptures on the site are untried. Most

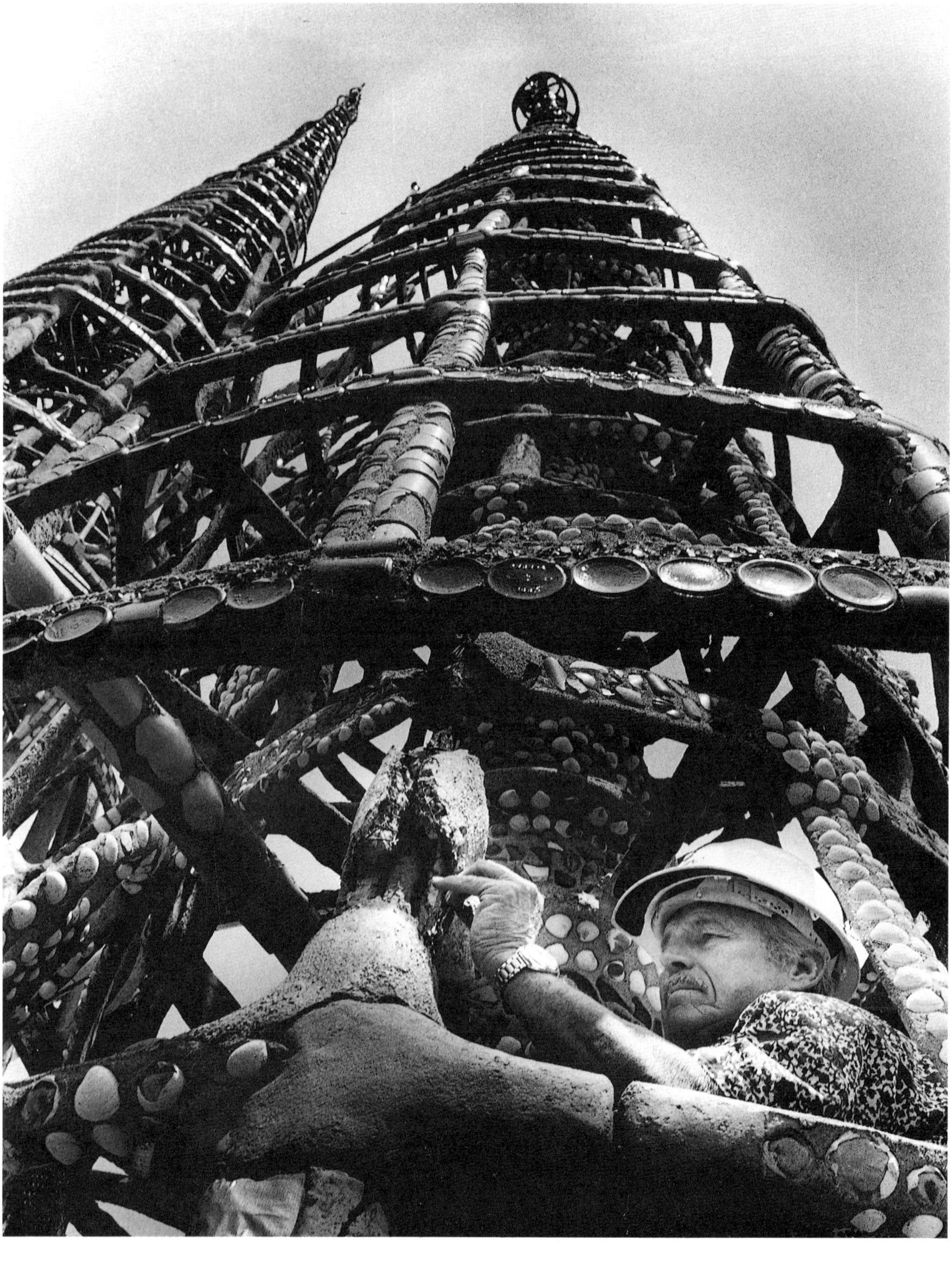

of these structures have not been repaired or treated for 20 years or more.

The superstructure over the Gazebo is 38 feet high and has not been inspected or repaired for 20 years. The Gazebo arched support columns are also severely cracked and pieces are subject to falling on those inside the sculpture.

The 27 feet tall chimney of Rodia's house is inadequately guy-wired (to other portions of the sculpture and to a fragile wall of the house) and suffers extreme structural damage at its main (and only) attachment to the base of the chimney.

A 20 feet tall spire at the east end of the site and the adjacent 28 feet tall mast of the ship have been denied inspection or repair for 2 decades and their structural condition is not known.

The hundreds of connecting members immediately over the heads of visitors as they walk through the site contain many serious cracks and loose pieces visible to the eye.

The decorated ceiling over the entrance to Rodia's house also contains cracks with the potential danger of falling pieces or parts and the condition of the large front wall of the house is suspect.

The types of threats to the structures may be viewed as gross or minute. A gross threat involves a potential major upset of one of the sculptures - due to wind or earthquake or settling of the foundation. A minute threat is a case of potential serious damage to the mortar cover and, later, to the metal mesh and reinforcements which may originate from a small crack in a mortar cover.

A satisfactory inspection program must quickly identify each type of threat and provide for timely corrective actions. Gross threats may be monitored by inspections for any movement of the structures, particularly after high winds and earthquakes. Minute threats may be monitored through a periodic, detailed visual survey of each supporting portion of each of the sculptures. Periodic checking for failures in the waterproofing must be accomplished, also. Priority must be assigned to the repair work and the work should begin as soon as possible. Thousands of repair photographs must be cataloged to establish an historic file or repairs which has been initiated to begin assessing the time between failures for repairs of various types since 1979, for use in cost estimations for future maintenance.

Although the State crews photographed each area of repair during the 74 month program, the quality of the photos and the lack of descriptions of the materials used and the work done, and the absence of photos of the "after" condition will handicap their future use in understanding which were used.

FUTURE PLANS

The International Forum for the Future of Sam Rodia's Towers in Watts.

A five year plan and schedule will be developed and updated to serve as a guide to near term repairs, inspection of completed repairs and other areas of the sculptures, and long term plans.

There have been widely differing opinions on the question of restoration versus conservation (or preservation) of the Rodia Towers.

Some believe the Towers should be "restored" to their previous state at a particular time in their history. Others believe the Towers should be conserved (preserved) as they are now. They have suffered great losses in decorative elements due to vandalism, aging, and the recently completed structural repair work by the State of California. Why not put substitute pieces into the mortar to simulate the missing sea shells, tiles, and bits of glass and pottery? In fact, the Ehrenkrantz report had approved the replacement of glass and tile and other decorative elements during the work just completed by the State. Daily reports in 1985 show the purchases of tile and glass by the crew, but no notes have been found as to where the substitute materials were placed.

Art authorities are opposed to this idea and quote the International Charter of Conservation which say: "Alteration of the original surface of a work of art should always be avoided. No action or procedure can justify the replacement, destruction or covering of the original surface...The elements used to replace missing parts..should not imitate the monument either in its artistic appearance or in its historic aspect...should always be recognizable and represent the minimum necessary to assure that the conservation of the monument restores the continuity of the sculptural form."

APPENDIX B

RESOLUTIONS OF THE INTERNATIONAL FORUM FOR THE FUTURE OF SAM RODIA'S TOWERS IN WATTS, DAVIDSON CONFERENCE CENTER, UNIVERSITY OF SOUTHERN CALIFORNIA, JUNE 13-15, 1985

WHEREAS: We the participants in the International Forum, held under the auspices of the Watts Towers Community Trust, representing a broad cross section of Watts Community Organizations; Los Angeles City, County, and State elected public officials; cultural institutions; colleges; universities; and experts in architectural and art conservation, urban design, education, economic and health services, from around the nation and abroad...and

WHEREAS: We did intensively discuss diverse aspects of Watts Towers preservation, conservation, maintenance, and security; the responsibilities, obligations, rights and duties of the concerned public agencies; and the desires, hopes and expectations of the Watts community and concerned citizens throughout the world...and

WHEREAS: Participants in the Forum did thoroughly discuss diverse aspects of the neighborhood's needs and desires regarding revitalization and environmental enhancement, including access to Watts Towers by road and rail and the links to other neighborhood social services, educational and cultural facilities...and

WHEREAS: The Forum believes that with appropriate resources and dedicated communication of the need to support the conservation of Watts Towers and the revitalization of its host community, much action will be accomplished to alleviate negative stereotypes associated with Watts...and

WHEREAS: The participants are committed to act affirmatively to achieve these goals and objectives by actively advocating, advising, consulting, and working to raise funds, promote and conserve Watts Towers and strengthen the community...and

WHEREAS: It is understood that 15th District Council Woman, Joan Milke Flores, has introduced a motion in the Los Angeles City council to conduct a comprehensive study to determine the future needs of Watts Towers and the adjacent Watts Towers Arts Center, "a cultural enrichment for our entire city", and to provide interim funding for the city's takeover of Watts Towers from the State Department of Parks and Recreation on July 1, 1985...now

THEREFORE, BE IT RESOLVED: That we, the participants in the International Forum for the future of Sam Rodia's Towers in Watts, do endorse Councilwoman Flores' motion before the Los Angeles City Council, and all further action and support of Watts Towers and its host community...and

FURTHER BE IT RESOLVED: That Forum participants believe that the newly formed Watts Towers Community Trust and its Community Advisory Council should be recognized by the City and county of Los Angeles and the State of California as the appropriate vehicles through whose agency the community and Watts Towers can best achieve the goals of revitalization and conservation respectively...and

FURTHER BE IT RESOLVED: That the participants recommend that the Office of the Mayor, in concert with the Los Angeles City Council, direct the Department of City Planning to work with the Watts Towers Community Trust and its Community Advisory Council to immediately bring together all responsible public agencies, including: Cultural Affairs, Public Works, General Services, Department of Real Estate, Recreation and Parks, Traffic and Transportation and all other pertinent City, County, and State agencies related to Watts Towers and the surrounding community, for the purpose of consolidating all current plans, actions, proposals, or operations which have, or will have, an impact on Watts Towers and its host community.

DATED: June 15, 1985

FORUM PANELISTS

Thirty-three panelists attending the International Forum for the Future of Sam Rodia's Towers in Watts included:

Co-chairmen:
Robet Harris, Dean USC School of Architecture.
Michael Pittas, Dean, Otis/Parsona AA Institute.

Watts Community Leaders:
Dr. Clyde Oden, Director, Watts Health Foundation.
Dr. Grace Payne, Executive Director, Westminster Neighborhood Association.
John Outterbridge, Director, Watts Towers Arts Center.
Ted Watkins, Director, Watts Labor Community Action Committee.

Los Angeles City Officials:
Pat Russell, President, Los Angeles City Council.
Joan Milke Flores, Councilwoman. L.A. City 15th District.
Edward Helfeld, Director, Community Redevelopment Agency.
Alan Sieroty, President, L.A. Cultural Affairs Commission.

California State Assembly and Senate Members:
William Greene State Senator.
Maxine Waters, State Assemblywoman.
U.S. Congressman:
Augustus Hawkins.

Los Angeles Architects, Artists and Art Professionals:
Richard Koshalek, Director, Museum of Contemporary Art.
Charles Moore, Architect.
Robert Kennard, Architect.
Jon Jerde, Architect.
Judith Baca, Artist.
Betye Saar, Artist.
Christopher Knight, Art Critic, L.A. Herald Examiner.
Leon Whiteson, L.A. Herald Examiner.

Developers:
Robert Maguire, President, Maguire, Thomas Partners.
Channing Johnson, President, Economic Resources Corporation.

Trade Union Representative:
William Robertson, Executive Secretary Treasurer, Los Angeles County Federation of Labor, AFL-CIO.

Preservationists, Historians and Engineers:

Martin Weil, President, Los Angeles Conservancy.
N.J. Goldstone, Engineer.
Regula Campbell, Architectural Historian.

National and International Participants:
Richard Meier, Architect, New York.
Lawrence Halprin, Urban Landscape Designer, San Francisco.
Diana Balmori, Architect and Urbanist, New Haven, Conn.
David Lee, Architect and Urban Designer, New York City.
Kenneth Greenberg, Director, Urban Design Group, Toronto City Council, Canada.
Ricardo Legorreta, Architect and Urbanist, Mexico City, Mexico.
Charles Correa, Architect, Bombay, India.

Appendix C

Chronology: of the Watts Towers, 1921-1987

1921, 1923:

Dates inscribed in Towers by Rodia as the beginning of his occupation of 1765-7 107th Street in the Unincorporateddistrict of Watts, Country of Los Angeles, and the start of the Towers' construction. Actual date of start may be later, possibly 1927.

1926, MAY:

Watts district annexed by the city of Los Angeles.

1948:

Reports indicate that Rodia has finished principal work in the Towers. Next 5-6 years devoted to maintenance and repair.

1954:
>Rodia deeds Towers to neighbor, Louis Sauceda, and leaves Los Angeles to join family in Martinez, California.

1957:
FEB. 5:
>L.A. City Department of Building and Safety issues demolition order against Towers as "unsafe structure."

SPRING:
>Sauceda sells Towers to Joseph Montoya for $1,000.00.

1959:
MAY:
>Montoya, unable to gain official permit to turn the Towers into a Taco stand, sells the Towers to William Cartright and Nicholas King for $3,000.00.

SUMMER:
>Cartwright and King transfer ownership of Towers newly created Committee for Simon Rodia's Towers in Watts (CSRTW), formed to protect Towers and raise donations for its maintenance and repair.

JULY, 6-23:
>CSRTW Attorney Jack Levine defends structural integrity of Towers at L.A. City demolition hearings.

OCTOBER:
>Structural test designed by Aerospace Engineer N.J. "Bud Goldstone" proves Towers structural strength and safety to city's satisfaction.

1963, MARCH:
>Towers declared a historical monument by L.A. City Heritage Board, and achieves listing on the National Register of Historic Places.

1965:
AUGUST:
>Civil revolt in Watts results in widespread destruction of nearby properties, but leaves Towers untouched.

JULY 16:
>Rodia dies in Martinez.

1966-7:
>CSRTW contstructs Watts Towers Arts Center, funded by private donations.

1975, OCT.24:
>CSRTW donates Towers to the City of Los Angeles. L.A. City Dept. of Public Works fail to carry out needed repairs.

1977, APRIL:
>Federal Housing and Urban Development agency (HUD) grants $250,000.00 to Towers under section 106 of the National Historic Preservation Act. L.A. City Dept. of Public Works still fails to carry out needed repairs.

1978:
MARCH 3:
>Long-neglected Towers closed "for reasons of public safety."

APRIL 28:
>State of California Bureau of Parks and Recreation awards City of Los Angeles $207,000.00 for Towers' restoration and repair.

MAY 19:
>City of L.A. deeds Towers to State, on 50-Year leaseback provision.

AUGUST 9:
>Architect Ralph Vaughn authorized to proceed with Phase I of Restoration Plan for Towers.

SEPT. 15:
>CSRTW, perturbed about quality of restoration work, engages Center for Law in the Public Interest to initiate litigation against City of L.A. .

1979:
OCT 4:

    State suspends restoration program.

SPRING:

    Small park established between Towers and adjacent Arts Center.

MAY:

    California office of State Architect develops conservation and maintenance plan for Towers. CSRTW Chairperson Jeanne Morgan complains publicly about "severe consequences of prolonged neglect" to Towers.

1980:
JULY 24:

    State grant funds of $207,000.00 for emergency repairs to Towers almost exhausted.

JULY 30:

    Bill AB 990, Appropriating $1,000,000.00 for Towers restoration and repair, approved by California State Assembly.

1981, OCT.:

    San Francisco-based The Ehrenkrantz Group (TEG) awarded contract for Towers' conservation study and maintenance report.

1984:

    TEG releases preservation plan and maintance and restoration guide for Towers.

1985:
FEB.:

    Watts Towers Community and Conservation Trust (WTCCT) formed to expedite settlement of seven-year lawsuit initiated by Center for Law in the Public Interest.

APRIL:

    Los Angeles Herald Examiner prints series of major articles dramatizing the plight of the Towers.

JUNE 13-15:
> The International Forum for the Future of Rodia's Towers in Watts is held at University of Southern California.

OCT. 29:
> Settlement of lawsuit No. 259603 signed by Center for Law in the Public Interest and the City of Los Angeles. Settlement calls for $800,000.00, five-year restoration and maintenance program for Towers.

OCTOBER:
> Towers Conservation Conference held under AEGIS of L.A. City Cultural Affairs Department.

NOVEMBER:
> State crews exhaust budget of 74-month repair program for Towers.

DECEMBER:
> N. J. "Bud" Goldstone appointed Technical Consultant for Tower by L.A. City Cultural Affairs Dept.

1986:
MARCH:
> Release of Watts Towers Conservation Handbook, outlining five-year program, drafted for Towers' restoration and maintenance.

OCTOBER:
> Photographer Marvin Rand contracted to prepare photographic baseline documentation record of Towers.

Appendix D

Bibliography

Books

Material Related to Rodia or the Towers

Babitz, Eve. Eve's Hollywood. (Los Angeles: Delacorte Press, 1972).

Bryan, Robert. Go Build Me a Tower. (Djai, CA: Topa Topa Enterprises Ltd., 1973).

Committee for the Preservation of Simon Rodia's Towers in Watts. The Watts Towers: Creativity, Play and Technology. (Los Angeles: Pacific Design Center, February, 1981). Photographic exhibit catalogue.

Jackson, William. "At the Grave of Simon Rodia" in Noel Alvin Gardner, ed. Streaks of Light. (California: New Dawn Publications, 1974).

Kalish, Richard A. The Psychology of Human Behaviour. (Belmont, CA:, 1966). Includes photographs of the Towers as an example of "healthy creativity."

Krasne, Lucille and Patty Zeitlin. Castle in My City. (San Carlos, CA: Golden Gate Junior Books, 1968).

Laporte, Paul M. The Man, The Work. (Los Angeles: Los Angeles County Museum, C. 1962). Exhibition catalogue.

Los Angeles County Museum of Art. Simon Rodia's Watts Towers. (Los Angeles: Los Angeles County Museum, 1965).

Laughlin, Clarence John. "A Pleasure Done in Los Angeles" in John Hadfield, ed., The Saturday Book. (London: Hutchinson Co., 1967). Pages 104-115.

Madian, Jon. Beautiful Junk: A Story of the Watts Towers. (Boston: Little Brown and Co., 1968). Fictionalized account of the relationship Rodia may have had with neighborhood children.

Rodman, Seldén. "The Artist Nobody Knows" New World Writing No. 2. (:Mentor Series, 1952).

Rolle, Andrew. The Immigrant Upraised: Italian Adventures and Colonists in an Expanding America. (:University of Oklahoma Press, 1968). Excerpt on Rodia

Rosen, Seymour. In Celebration of Ourselves. (San Francisco: California Living book, 1979). Also title of exhibit held at San Francisco Museum of Modern Art December 3, 1976 to January 23, 1977.

Seeworker, Joseph. Nuestro Pueblo: Los Angeles, City of Romance. (Boston: Houghton, Mifflin Co., 1940). Item on "Glasstowers and Demon Rodia."

Background Material

Banham, Reyner. Los Angeles, The Architecture of Four Ecologies. (New York: Harper and Row, 1971).

Bishop, Robert Charles. American Folk Sculpture. (New York: E.P. Dutton & Co., 1974).

Borne, Alain. Le Facteur Cheval. (Paris: R. Morcel, 1969).

Bowron, Fletcher. Los Angeles and Its Environs in the Twentieth Century. (Los Angeles: Ward Ritchie Press, 1976).
Bullock, Paul Watts, the Aftermath: An Inside View of the Ghetto by the People of Watts. (New York: Grove Press, 1969).

Casanelles, E. Nueva Vison de Gaudi. (Barcelona: La Poligrafa, 1965).

Casson, Sir Hugh Maxwell. Follies. (London: Chatto and Windus, Ltd., 1963).

Collins, Keith. Black Los Angeles, the Maturing of the Ghetto (Los Angeles: Century Twenty-one Publishing, 1980).

Davenport, William. Art Treasures of the West. (Menlo Park, CA: Lane Magazine and Book Co., 1966).

Friedman, Michael. Les Secrets du Facteur Cheval. (Paris: J.C. Simoen, 1977).

Inoya, Beata. The Three Worlds of Los Angeles. (United States Information Service and Cultural Centers in Europe, 1974). Exhibit catalogue.

Jakovsky, Anatole. Damonen and Wunder. (Cologne: Verlag M. DuMont Schauberg, 1963).

Jones, Barbara. Follies and Grottos. (London: Constable, 1949, revised 1974).

Lancaster, Clay. Follies: Architectural Follies in America. (Rutland, VT: C.E. Tuttle Co., 1960).

Lipman, Jean. American Folk Art in Wood, Metal and Stone. (New York: Pantheon Books, 1948).

Lipke, William C. Clarence Schmidt. (Burlington, VT: The Robert Hull Fleming Museum, December 1974).

Porter, Tom. How Architects Visualize. (New York: Van Nostrand Co., 1979).

Quimby, Ian M.G. and Scott Swank, eds. Perspectives in American Folk Art. (New York: C.E. Norton Co., 1980).

Robinette, Margaret. Outdoor Sculpture: Object and Environment. (New York: Whitney Library of Design, 1976).

Rudofsky, Bernard. Architecture Without Architects. (New York: Doubleday Inc., 1964).

Seitz, W.C. The Art of Assemblage. (New York: Museum of Modern Art, 1961).

Somner, Robert. Mudflat Sculpture. (Davis, CA: University of California, September, 1979).

, Street Art. (New York: Links Books, 1975).

Walker Art Center. Naives and Visonaries. (Minneapolis: Walker Art Center, 1974).

Watts Writers Workshop. From the Ashes: Voices of Watts. (New York: New Americna Library, 1967).

Wolfram, Eddie. History of Collage: An Anthology of Collage, Assemblage and Event Structures. (New York: MacMillan & Co., 1975).

Young, Joseph L. Course in Making Mosaics. (New York: Reinhold Publishing Co., 1957).

MAGAZINE ARTICLES

Magazines

"A Dream in Steel." Now 69. (March 1969).

"American Heritage." Newsweek. (April 1, 1963).

American Institute of Architect, Southern California Chapter. Bulletin. (May 5, 1957).

American Institute of Graphic Arts. Design and Printing of the Year. (No. 83, 1963). Photographic exhibition catalogue designed by Allen Porter using Towers selected as one of best of year.

"Art groups fight to save L.A. Towers: Bizarre Structure in Suburban Watts." Architectural Forum 111 (July 1959): 9-11.

Banham, Rayner. "The Spec Builders on Trial–Towards a Pop Architecture," Architectural Review (July 1962): 44.

Barr, Alfred Jr. "Homage to Sam," Art Forum (July 20, 1965).

Barry, L. "Legacy of Simon Rodia," Popular Photography 59 (October 1966): 34.

Ben-Torim, Grace. "A Line On Our Friends," The Municipal Guardian 1 (November 1961).

Billiter, Bill. "Simon Rodia's Incredible Towers," Art News (April 1979): 92-95.

Bryan, Robert and Jack Smith. "Simon Rodia and the Children of Watts," Westways (1970).

Chase-Marshall, Janet. "The Fight to Save the Watts Towers," US (June 13, 1978): 32-33.

"Civilization Wins a Round," Architectural Forum 118 (April 1963):81.

Conrads, Ulrich. "Phantastiche architektur Unterstomungen in er architecktur des 20 jahrhunderts," Zodiac (1959): 117-37.

Craven, John. "Les Tours de Watts," Connaissance des Arts 170 (Avril 1966): 110-113.

Cunliffe, H.J. "Report to the Board of Building and Safety Commissioners on Wind Forces as Applied to Framed Towers." Journal of the Structural Division, Proceedings of the American Society of Civil Engineers." Papers No. 1707-1712(July 1958).

"Death of an Enigma," Architectural Forum. (September 1965): 19.

de Nees, Robert. "Lost Angeles," National Geographic 122(1962):483.

"Die Turm von Watts," Werk 55(March 68): 192-93.

"Don't Forget the Story of Simon Rodia," Look Magazine (June 28, 1966): 54.

Edelstein, Eleanor. "The Watts Towers," Coastlines 6(September 1964): 52ff.

"Fantasy in Steel, Concrete and Broken Bottles." Arts and Architecture. 76(September 1959): 27-28.

Genauer, Emily. "Grassroots Art from Fertile Soil." Newsday. (January 29, 1975).

"Gli Straordinaire Torre di Watts." Domus. (December 1951): 264-65.

Goldstone, Norman J. "Structural Test of a Hand-Built Tower." Experimental Mechanics. (January 1963): 8-13.

Goldstone, Penelope S. "Watts Towers Show Structural Capacity of Lathing." Progressive Architecture. 41(April 1960): 190-93.

Gould, Max, trans. "Monumento Gigante Hecho con Chatarra se Convierte en Obra Mastra de Arte." La Prensa. (February 23, 1964).

"Home is Where You Make It." Horizon. VI(Autumn) 1964): 114ff.

Kirkby, Eleanor. "Center for a Culture." Art Calendar. (December-January 1968): 26-27.

Knud, Abell. "Watts Towers." Arkitekten. 61(December 29,1959): 488.

"Labyrinth of Watts." Time Magazine. 58(September 3, 1951): 80ff.

Langsner, Jules. "Contemporary Art and City Hall in Los Angeles: Controversy over the Fantastic Towers of Watts." Art News. 58(September 1959): 49.

. "Sam of Watts: I had in my mind to do something big and I did." Arts and Architecture. 58(July 1951): 23-25.

. Craft Horizon. XIX(November, December 1959): 6.

. Westways. (October 1959).

Lapham, Lewis H. "The Great Idea Boy." Saturday Evening Post. (February 13, 1965): 74-79. Article on fashion designer Rudi Geurnrich, using Towers as backdrop for photographs.

Laughlin, Clarence. "The Watts Towers." Vogue. 13(February 1961).

"Le Torre di Watts." Panorama. No. 29(Febraio 1965): 86-93.

Longstreet, Stephen. "Simon Rodia's Masterpiece" and "Sam Got Away Just in Time..." From KPFK Program Folio, August 30 and September 12, 1965. Reprinted in "In Memoriam Simon Rodia." Free Press. (July 23, 1965): 5.

McWilliams, C. "Watts: The Forgotten Slum." Nation. 201(August 30, 1965): 90.

Mendelsohn, Georges. "Un petit American tranquille a construit seul une cathedral insolite." Reforme. 16(September 1961): 8-9.

"Miraculous Madness of Simon Rodia." Apollo. 78(September 1963): 236-37.

Neville, Emily. "The Name is Simon Rodia." Beginnings. (1968):70-71.

"New Look by New Breed." Sepia. 19(September 1968). Fashion article using Towers as backdrop.

"Oh Brother, Only in L.A." Los Angeles, Magazine of the Good Life in Southern California. (September 1961): 2.

Oyama, Mary. "The Watts Towers, Artistry or Oddity?" The Rafu-Shimpo Supplement. (December 1966): 10.

Redington, Michael. "The Establishment of the Pillar." The Manchester Guardian. (August 17, 1965).

Read, Penelope. "Die Watts Towers." Du/Atlantis. 26(October 1965): 2, 780-86.

"Religion." Time Magazine. (July 4, 1969): 57. Towers used as location of religious ceremony.

Ring, Douglas. "Simon Rodia and His Towers." Aloft. (January-March 1970).

Robin, Marianne. "The Tiled Towers: Simon Rodia's Monumental Artwork." Tile and Decorative Surfaces. (May-June 1979).

"Rodia Revisited." Los Angeles, Magazine of the Good Life in Southern California. (February 1962): 14-15.

"Rodia's Towers, Monument to One Man's 13 Years' Preoccupation with Trivia." Bruce Magazine. (E. Bruce & Co., Memphis, Tennessee), 41(Winter 1960-61).

Royston, Landau. "Watts Towers. Arkitekten. 61(December 29,1959): 488.

"Sam of Watts." Architectural Review. 111(March 1952): 201-03.

"See One Man's Great Folk Art, Rodia Towers." Parents' Magazine. (December 1961): 137.

Silverman, Ronald H. "Watts, The Disadvantaged and Art Education." Art Education Magazine. 19(March 1966): 17.

Silvy, Maurice. "Les Trous de Watts de Simon Rodilla." Aujourd'hui. (June 8, 1958).

"Simon Rodia's strangely beautiful monument to his city." Lincoln Log. (Lincoln Savings and Loan Assoc.) (October 1962): 2,6.

"Simone Rodia: un artista irpino." Roma. (Agosto 9, 1972).

Steinitz, Kate T. "A Visit with Sam Rodia." Architectural Forum. 1(May 1963): 32-33.

. "Fantastic Architecture." Art Forum. (August 1962).

. "Fantistic Architecture: The Simon Rodia Towers of Watts." L'Arte Milan. (October-December 1959).

. "Simon Rodia's Tuerme von Watts." Neue Zeuercher Zeitung. (January 30, 1960).

. "The Destruction of the Watts Towers Attempted." Press Release, Santa Barbara Museum, c. 1959.

. "Towers in Jeopordy?" DMA; Downey Museum of Art Journal. (October 1959).

"Strange Test of a Magic Towers." The Engineer of Southern California.

18(December 1965): 17. Announcement of lecture by N.J. Goldstone.

"Tours de Watts L.A." L'Architecture d'Aujourd'hui. 35(Juin-Juillet 1962): 27.

"The Wonderful Towers of Sabatino Rodia." Sunset Magazine. 118(February 1957): 5.

"Toppling Towers." Newsweek. 54(July 20, 1959): 57.

Trillin, Calvin. "I Know I Want to Do Something." The New Yorker. 41(May 29, 1965): 72ff.

. "U.S. Journal: The Towers of Watts." The New Yorker. (December 4, 1971): 136-43.

"Un italiano nella L.A. amara." il Architettara. 5(January 1960): 579.

Willoughby. "Watts Towers." Ameryka. (published in Polish by the U.S. Information Agency) No. 13(1959): 2. Also No. 24(1960): 2.

"Watts Towers." Conoisseur. 191(April 1976): 388.

INDEX

Alberobello, 25
Alexander, Angie, 11, 16
Angelina, 12
Architecture Without Architects, 25
Art Center, 49
Arts & Architecture, 24
Assembly Bill 990, 28, 85

Barov, Zdravko, 28
Barrelhouse, 38, 61
Batchelder, Ernest, 42, 23
Batchelder Tile Company, 42
Batchelder-Wilson, 42
Belvedere Junior High, 52
Berendo Junior High, 53
Billy Berg's, 63
Bontemps, Arna, 33
Bottle, 7-UP, 15, 23, 41, 56, 67
Bradley, Mayor Tom, 5, 20, 34, 38
Bronowski, Dr. Joseph, 24
Bruno, Giordano, 17
Bryan, Robert S., 15, 87, 90
Byer, Mary Lou, 18
Byer, Brad, 13, 16, 24, 25

Cactus gardens, 24
Calicura, Nick, 20, 22
Cartwright, William, 26, 83
Caruso, Enrico, 15
Carver Junior High, 53
Carver, Norman, 25
Center For Law In The Public Interest, 28, 84, 86
Center tower, 22, 44, 75
Central Avenue, 32, 38
Charcoal Alley, 32
Cherryland Black Dot McGhee's, 61
Cheval, Ferdinand, 24
Chevrolet Division, 36
Chew-Moore, Birdell, 38
Childhood, 10
City of Los Angeles, 28, 49, 57, 68, 71, 73, 79, 80, 84, 86
Civil revolt, 83
Clark, Sir Kenneth, 20
Club Alabam, 38, 61, 63
Coggins, Bill, 37

Colacurcio, Frank, 18
Colacurcio, Sam, 12, 18
Colette, Buddy, 38
Committee for Simon Rodia's Towers, 27, 67, 69, 72, 83, 87
Committtee, 28
Community Advisory Council, 80

Compton, 14, 33
Conservation Handbook, 86
Conservation, 67, 71
Conservation and Maintenance Plan, 69, 73
Conservation Conference, 86
CSRTW, 84
Cultural Heritage Monument, 41

Daiser Permanente Watts Counselling & Learning Center, 37
Davis, Jack, 16
Davis, Sarah, 16
Department of Parks and Recreation, 28
Department of City Planning, 80
Department of Building and Public Safety, 74
Dept. of Public Works, 84
Disturbances in August 1965, 33
Down Beat, 63

Earl, Paris, 37, 40
East tower, 44, 75
East tower, 57-foot, 22
Ehrehkrantz Group (The), 28-9, 67, 69, 75, 78, 85
El Rancho Tijuata, 32
Experimental Mechanics,, 27

Festa de Gigli, 24
Flores, Joan Milke, 15th District Council Woman, 32, 80, 81
Forum, 80
Fruitvale, 12, 55
Fuller, Buckminster, 20, 21

Gaudi, Antonio, 7, 16
Gazebo, 9, 43-4, 73, 75, 77
Getty, J. Paul, Trust, 28
Gillespie, Dizzy, 63
Gladding McBean and Co., 42
God Send Sunday, 33
Goldstone, Norman J. "Bud", 27-8, 82, 83, 86, 91
Gompers Junior High, 53

Hacienda Village, 34
Hale Junior High, 53
Hale, William, 24
Harte Preparatory Intermediate, 53
Hollenbeck Junior School, 53
Hollier, Waren, 28
Human Relations Commissions, 36

Imperial Courts, 34, 36
Int'l Congress of Architects & Technicians of Monuments, 28
International Forum, 79
International Forum for the Future of Rodia's Towers in Watts, 86
International Charter of Conservation, 79
Italian Hilltowns, 25

J. Paul Getty Museum, 69, 73
Jack's Basket, 63
Johnson, Freda Shaw, 38
Jordan Downs, 34, 37

King Junior High, 53
King, Nicholas, 26, 83
Knight, Christopher, 81

L.A. City Dept. of Public Works. 84
L.A. City Heritage, 83
L.A. City Cultural Affairs Dept., 86
Langsner, Jules, 24, 91
Last Work, 63
Lawrence, D.H., 25
Leiber, Jerry, 61-3
Lockheed Watts-Willowbrook plant, 36
Long Beach, 13
Long Beach Quake, 1933, 15, 22
Los Angeles Building and Safety Department, 20, 69, 72
Los Angeles City Council, 80
Los Angeles Herald Examiner, 85
Los Angeles County Museum of Art, 87
Los Angeles Times, 17
Los Angeles City Building and Safety Department, 27, 44, 83
Los Angeles Cultural Heritage Board, 28
Los Angeles Unified School District, 52
Lovejoy, 63

Maintenance and Restoration Guide, 69, 75
Malibu Potteries, 42
Malibu tiles, 23, 42
Manley, Harold, 27
Martin Luther King Hospital, 49
Martinez, 11, 18, 20, 83, 84
Maye, Mary Alice, 33, 34
McCone Commission, 1965, 36
Memo, 63

Mid-City Alternative Junior High, 53
Milk of Magnesia, 15, 23, 41, 56
Millikan Junior High, 53
Mingus, Charles, 38, 47, 59, 63
Monk, Thelonius, 59
Montoya, Joseph, 83
Montoya, Louis, 26
Moore, Charles, 7, 81
Morgan, Jeanne, 20, 85
Mudtown, 33
Muir Junior High, 53
Murphy, Eddie, 40
Museum of Contemporary Arts, 52
National Trust for Historic Preservation, 69, 73
National Trust of the United States, 41
National Register of Historic Places, 28, 83
Nervi, Luigi, 22
Nickerson Gardens, 34, 36
Nola, 24
Nuestro Pueblo, 5, 9, 15, 17, 56, 57
Nuraghi, 26

Olamina, Babalade, 38
Otis, Johnny, 38, 60-1, 63
Outterbridge, John, 32, 40, 49, 81

Pacific Electric Red Cars, 32
Parker, Charlies "Bird", 59, 63
Peck, James, 13
Phillips, Esther, 38, 61
Poverty, 34
Powell, Bud, 59
Pryor, Richard, 40

Rabeneck, Andrew, 29
Rand, Marvin, 86
Registry of Historic Places, 41
Report by the L.A. Dept. of City Planning, 36
Revolt, 1965, 28, 31, 34, 49
Riot, 31

Rivotoli, 11, 56
Roach, Max, 59
Rodia Joint, 22
Rodia, Lucy, 12
Rodia, Tony, 16
Rodia, Frank, 12
Rodia, Benita, 13
Rodia, Simon, 41
Rodia, Alfred, 12, 18
Rodia, Fred, 18
Rodilla, Simon, 17, 41
Rodman, Selden, 14
Rose, Tokyo, 17
Rudofsky, Bernard, 25

Sauceda, Louis, 26, 83
Saucedo, Robert, 37
Savoy, 63
Schulberg, Budd, 38
Schwitters, Kurt, 25
Sea and Sardinia, 25
Seattle, 12, 55
Seitz, William, 21
Ship of Marco Polo, 24, 44, 75
Simon Rodia Art Center, 47
South-Central Area Welfare Planning, 36
St. Sebastian, 17
State of California Bureau of Parks & Recreation awards 84
State Department of Parks and Recreation, 69, 73, 75, 80
State of California, 28, 67, 69, 73, 75, 78, 80
State Architect, 29, 69, 72, 73, 85
Steinitz, Kate, 27, 93
Stoller, Mike, 61-63
Street East, 107th, 1765-69, 14, 43

Tajuata, 32
The Art of Assemblage, 21
The Cry of Christian Freedom, 16

The Ascent of Man, 24
The Herald Examiner, 52
Towers Mainenance and Restoration Guide, 28
Trillin, Calvin, 18, 25, 26, 94

UC Berkeley, 25
Ucci, Lucy, 12
Unemployment, 34

Vaughn, Ralph A., 28, 84
Vernon and Bauer pottery works, 23
Virgil Junior High, 53

Walker, T-Bone, 38, 61, 63
Waters, Maxine, 38, 81
Watkins, Ted, 36, 81
Watts Station, 33
Watts Train Station, 10
Watts Community Development Action Committee, 33
Watts Shopping Center, 33, 34
Watts Labor Community Action Committee, 36
Watts Manufacturing Corp., 36
Watts Towers Community Trust, 79, 80
Watts Writers Workshop, 38
Watts Health Center, 38
Watts Towers Community and Conservation Trust, 85
Watts, Charles H., 32
Watts, 5, 7, 13, 14-18, 33-4, 36-38, 40, 55-6, 59, 60-1, 63-5
Watts Tower Arts Center, 28, 32, 40, 47, 50
West tower, 22, 44, 75
Whiteson, Leon, L.A. Herald Examiner, 81
Wilmington Junior High, 53
Winged Victory, 23

Young People of Watts Improvement Center, 37